TREASURY

POSITIVE
ANSWERS

by Vernon Howard

911 Bryant Place
Ojai, California 93023-3301
805-640-2777
Fax: 805-640-2772

Copyright 1977 by Vernon Howard

New Life Edition 1990
4th Printing

ISBN 0-911203-21-4

Library of Congress Catalog Card Number 77-801005

Vernon Howard lives and teaches
in Boulder City, Nevada.
For information on books, tapes and classes write:
NEW LIFE
PO BOX 684
BOULDER CITY, NEVADA 89005
USA

CONTENTS

1. Start Exploring Your New World   7

2. Make Swift and Pleasant Progress   23

3. Take Command in Human Relations   39

4. How to Win Higher Guidance   56

5. Abolish Heartache and Regret   73

6. Mental Magic for Real Riches   90

7. Gain True Power and Energy   106

8. Answers to Baffling Questions   123

9. How to Change Who You Are   139

10. Pearls for Your Cosmic Treasury   55

11. Be Secure in an Anxious World   171

12. Boldly Venture and Conquer   187

ABOUT THE AUTHOR   204

HOW TO USE THIS BOOK

This book presents the great truths of the ages in simple language, using the popular question and answer method. The goal is self-enrichment and the result is new life-command. You will discover practical plans for traveling from where you are to where you really want to be. The questions are typical of those asked at the author's own lectures and classes.

The following steps will supply rich results: 1. On your first reading, cover the questions and answers casually and lightly. Let the first healthy impressions penetrate as they wish. 2. On your second reading write down the numbers of the items of special interest. Review and ponder these outstanding items. 3. Use the book in classes and study groups. Volunteers can read selected items aloud and comment on them for the benefit of all. Also, the class leader can read an item aloud and direct the group in open discussion.

Remember, the knowledge in these pages exists already in your higher nature. You need only ascend to its location within yourself. Real wisdom has been compared to a vast treasure located on a mountain peak. Will we climb? Will we continue to climb in spite of all obstacles? If so, the treasure is ours. So start the fascinating adventure right now.

Vernon Howard
Boulder City, Nevada

Chapter 1

START EXPLORING YOUR NEW WORLD

1. Q: I wish to understand my self and my life.

A: That is one of the finest statements you could ever make. Understanding is everything, for you can never be hurt or frightened by an event which you really understand.

2. Q: It is good news to hear that we need not remain in our present state of defeat.

A: A captured soldier was thrown into a dungeon. There seemed to be no escape. But by diligent effort he found a secret passage not known by his captor. He followed it to liberty. Like that soldier, we can find the passage to inner freedom. It can be called God, Reality, Cosmic Wisdom or any other name we choose.

3. Q: We are all looking for something, not knowing what it is.

A: It is something which is not presently a solid part of your psychic system. That is why you cannot define it. Let this simple fact both explain and encourage. Your sensing of another world is quite correct, and with knowledgeable vigilance you will find it. Though you cannot presently see or describe the castle beyond the thick woods, it is definitely there.

4. Q: I am frightened by the idea of traveling through the forest in order to reach the castle. Who knows what dreadful mental dragons I may meet.

A: A dragon is nothing more than an idea, and a false idea at that. I have urged you to walk right up to a wild-eyed dragon and call its stupid bluff. But you must do this to see this.

5. Q: I am fascinated at the prospect of finding something real.

A: Fascination is the right word.

6. Q: In the past I have been grateful to the wrong people, such as those who agree with my errors. Now I am grateful to those who tell me the truth about myself, to anyone with real insight.

A: A man of true mental sight is like a small and unnoticed island of safety in humanity's troubled sea.

7. Q: I am convinced that most human lives are nothing more than a gigantic ache, carefully concealed from others.

A: There is something beyond the ache, which means you must do some traveling. It is really a lot more fun than you think.

8. Q: I am attracted to these teachings, but am uncertain about my ability to understand. Perhaps I should wait until I am more sure of myself.

A: Do you know what that is like? That is like saying you will not pick up a book until you have first learned to read! You need not wait another second to start doing truly good things for yourself. Take any idea you hear in class tonight. It is an open door for you right now. Walk through. Right now.

9. Q: How do these principles affect our daily activities?

A: They help in an astonishing way. A clear mind is a powerful mind. As a specific example, they increase internal efficiency so you are able to do much more in less time.

10. Q: How can we make a fresh start in life?

A: By seeing the difference between a false fresh start and a real one. For every person who makes a real fresh start there are millions who wrongly believe it means to move to another city or to get a new spouse or to change employment. A real fresh start consists of seeking something higher than the present ways of thinking and behaving.

11. Q: Spiritual literature describes man as lost. What does it mean to be lost?

A: It means to be separated from your real nature. It means to be a slave of your own angers and sorrows and delusions. It means to live egotistically while labeling it nobility. It means to lack knowledge of your real purpose on earth, which is to unite yourself with God, Truth, Reality.

12. Q: Why do we fail to return to our cosmic homeland?

A: Because you can tell a lost man all day long how lost he is and at the end of the day he will stand up and say, "I'm glad you were not describing *me!*"

13. Q: Show us how to take part in our own rescue.

A: Make a conscious effort to prefer wholeness over fragmentation. Make a deliberate attempt to choose essence over artificiality. Make an energetic endeavor to select transformation over repetition.

14. Q: I know there is something wrong with my life but don't know what it is.

A: Happily, at the start you need only know there is something wrong, which finally leads to insights and corrections.

15. Q: For many years I felt no need for these higher facts. I suppose that was part of my general delusion.

A: Those who feel no need for higher facts should examine what their lives are like without them.

16. Q: Where do seekers go wrong?

A: People can get very excited over a new

but false philosophy. They think they have changed themselves when they have merely substituted one delusion for another delusion. That is like praising a tiger for saving you from a lion. A sincere seeker wants rescuing facts, not flattering fantasies.

17. Q: Please supply an example of how self-knowledge leads to self-transformation.

A: Become aware, more aware, emotionally aware of how weary you are of your life as it now unfolds, for then a study of esoteric principles becomes the royal road to a different kind of life.

18. Q: So realization of our weariness is really an opportunity for self-refreshment?

A: The rare individual who realizes that his life is simply a mechanical imitation of everyone he has ever met will have an opportunity to become unique.

19. Q: When entering these studies for the first time I was scared at what I might see in myself, and am still somewhat frightened. Is this a common problem with beginners?

A: Always. This is simply the activity of negative imps who work hard to scare you away from your right course of seeing into yourself. Refuse to be intimidated by them. You are stronger than they. Everyone who has reached the Island of Reality once dared to enter the stormy seas of his own nature.

11

20.   Q: How can I start the spiritual journey?

A: Instead of simply suffering from yourself, study your suffering and yourself.

21.   Q: What do you mean by constructive dissatisfaction?

A: One student determined to be dissatisfied with three things. The first was to be dissatisfied with living as he had lived in the past. The second was to be dissatisfied with the childish toys of society. The third was to be dissatisfied with believing he already had the answers to life.

22.   Q: We seem to have everything backward.

A: Take inner exploration as an example. People feel there is danger in seeing themselves as they are, when in fact the danger resides in evading the actual condition. Self-exploration appears hazardous only as long as we continue to defend the old and stubborn nature. Safety comes with the ending of this psychic tyrant.

23.   Q: What would you say to someone new on the path?

A: A first step toward self-liberation is to realize deeply that every human being you meet is far more confused and afraid than he or she appears to be on the surface.

24.   Q: But this may drop us into despair over finding someone to guide us.

A: Instead, let it drop you onto that tremendous virtue seldom seen—reliance upon the natural cosmic forces which surely reside within you.

25. Q: Are there people on earth who really understand life?

A: A few. A man who really knows what life is all about is like a home which appears ordinary to passers-by, but which has a secret room containing an immense treasure.

26. Q: How can we find such a man?

A: Only an awakening love for truth within an individual can serve as a guide toward him. This means you can no longer go along with most people. In spite of what they tell you, most people prefer their artificial treasures, such as self-centeredness and fear of change.

27. Q: Are you saying that we *prefer* fear of change?

A: If you did not prefer fear of any kind you could not have it—or rather, it could not have you.

28. Q: That is a new idea to me. We love our unhappy states.

A: Try to see deeply into this human peculiarity. It will lead you upward. Remind yourself that one of man's problems is his unnatural fondness for negative feelings, like a strange sailor who loves stormy seas.

29. Q: Then some people are happy only when miserable!

A: Exactly. Look for examples of this among people.

30. Q: Why do we fail in our efforts to understand?

A: Life-in-error cannot be understood. There is nothing there to understand. Suppose a hypnotist makes an audience believe there is a fierce wolf in the room. In fear they try to escape the wolf, or fight it, appease it, or seek to understand it. It is all useless and tiring. But suppose they break the hypnotic spell? Where is the wolf to understand or fight?

31. Q: The stormy and senseless course of my life turned me toward books of higher ideas. At first they were more puzzling than enlightening, but gradually they became clear and refreshing. Is that the usual experience?

A: This delight comes to all persistent seekers. One tiny part of your psychic system ventured into new lands, which annoyed other reluctant parts. Gradually, this single right part gained authority over the weak parts, defeating their attempts to continue to cause confusion.

32. Q: It is astonishing how the very same words I had read a dozen times suddenly revealed new and profound messages.

A: Like to hear something equally astonishing? While you were reading the words in the book you were also reading your own higher viewpoints which had been released by a wish to learn.

33. Q: This class has made me clear to myself. I used to think I had inner poise, but now I see I have always been caught in the whirlpool of raging emotions.

A: Self-clarity is self-health. Those who have escaped the whirlpool are those who first suspected they were in this hazardous condition.

34. Q: I agree that society is a horror. It invites you to a masked ball, and at midnight the pleasant masks fall off. You are shocked to find yourself surrounded by human animals. The invitation is always a trap.

A: Then listen to the cosmic invitation. Truth invites, "Admit that you really do not know what your life is all about and I will help you to actually know."

35. Q: Sometimes the path seems so difficult to travel.

A: A student complained to his teacher about the long and hard journey toward the inner kingdom. The teacher informed, "Reduce your resistance to the kingdom and you reduce the distance to the kingdom."

36. Q: It seems we are even unable to distinguish between light and darkness.

A: Then ponder these helpful facts. Darkness is extremely cunning and persistent in masquerading as light. Light never really battles darkness, for any hostile battle is between two kinds of darkness. Light and darkness have nothing to do with each other. Light understands darkness, but darkness cannot understand light, though it insists it can. Light comes by personally perceiving the destructive nature of darkness.

37. Q: These teachings are so perfectly sensible I am surprised that they are so unappreciated.

A: The only mind capable of appreciating the sensibleness of higher teachings is a mind which has risen above its own nonsense acquired from a nonsensical society.

38. Q: Show us how to rise above the commonplace.

A: By seeking a bit more self-knowledge every day you do something far greater than conquering the entire world. This is not sentimental philosophy but a tremendous truth.

39. Q: I notice that many people are unhappy with their religion or their beliefs, yet hesitate to drop them in favor of workable principles. Why this hesitation?

A: They fear there may not be anything beyond their familiar but useless beliefs. Fearing that any new road might end in the wilderness, they fail to see they are already in the wilderness. There is something beyond the familiar. It is found by those who dare to depart from the habitual.

40. Q: I fear I may ask wrong questions.

A: If the attitude is right the question is never wrong. If the attitude is wrong the question is never right.

41. Q: I have a horror of facing fully something I have only glimpsed. I feel that my life and all its activities are meaningless, absolutely without purpose. Can you understand my terror at seeing any deeper into this? Do you understand what I am trying to say?

A: Perfectly. I am very glad for you. The horror of your life is becoming conscious for the first time. This is a good and necessary stage. Do not turn away from this horror, but study it with scientific interest. You are now on your way toward inner newness, so be very glad that this has happened to you.

42. Q: How does willingness help?

A: Be willing to be upset by truth in order to end the dreadful tyranny of delusion.

43. Q: Please define the meaning of consciousness.

A: It can be classified as simple consciousness and higher consciousness. Simple consciousness operates when you are aware of something through the five senses, such as seeing a river or hearing music. It also operates through memory and imagination, as when you remember how to spell or imagine how a new coat will look. It consists of ordinary thought, and is useful for daily activities.

Higher consciousness is just that—a much higher state.

44. Q: What is the nature of higher consciousness?

A: It is as different from simple consciousness as noon is different from midnight. It sees life without conditioned thought, which means it is free of both past and future. It lives casually in the present moment, the free moment. Being whole it has no compulsive need to prove itself, and therefore has no inner arguments or outer conflicts. Higher consciousness, cosmic consciousness, possesses authentic sanity and goodness.

45. Q: You were probably expecting this question, but how is higher consciousness attained?

A: By absorbing and acting upon everything you hear in these classes. But there is one point I want to emphasize above all else. No one can absorb and act as long as he takes simple consciousness as higher consciousness. Almost everyone makes this error, and not seeing it as an error *he thinks he already possesses the higher state*. This blocks all learning, all ascending. Never forget this.

46. Q: Please offer aids for avoiding this error.

A: See clearly that simple consciousness cannot uplift your inner condition. It has never conquered dread and tension and hostility and it never will. It can only cover them up, leaving you in a painful state of unconscious self-contradiction.

Even ordinary knowledge about religion and psychology changes nothing. Dare to take the leap beyond familiar thought. The cosmic country then appears.

47. Q: The meaning of life eludes me.

A: I will give you a sentence of just seven words which you should think about often. Only understanding can give meaning to life. I repeat. Only understanding can give meaning to life. So what must you acquire?

48. Q: We wish to gain real and lasting benefits. How?

A: You can win real rewards by learning the difference between real and false rewards—which few human beings know.

49. Q: We have many doubts we cannot even see.

A: I will tell you about one of the most subtle of all doubts. It attacks those who have taken the first few steps on the true path. It is the fear that this new way may also lead nowhere, may prove a disappointment. The doubt is like a huge gray cloud, but the sun of consciousness makes it disappear forever.

50. Q: You said that right encouragement consists of realization. What might we realize?

A: It is right encouragement to realize that no person and no circumstance can prevent Truth from performing its noble work within you. Not even your habitual nature can prevent it, provided you invite something that is not part of your habitual nature.

51. Q: Why do we have so little direction in life?
   A: Because it is so easy to drift, and most people want the easy way. They make no effort to change the direction of their days. They cling to their familiar reactions to life, resisting and resenting anyone who tries to show them their own deliverance. Direction comes by deliberately paddling upstream, by going against society's lazy flow.

52. Q: Specifically, how is direction developed?
   A: By voluntarily doing something difficult for you to do. A man resting in psychological dependence upon others could seek and find his own internal resources. A woman who is afraid of someone could question the necessity of her fear. Any start is a good start.

53. Q: We have so many strange ideas about the nature of the quest. I am still shedding them.
   A: Some people think they must journey to faraway temples in search of eternal wisdom. They can in fact sit in the center of a noisy business office and *be* eternal wisdom.

54. Q: Why is it so hard to convince us of these facts?
   A: A sparrow used to perch in a barren but favorite tree on the prairie, which gave him a

feeling of familiarity and safety. One day he returned to find the tree toppled by the wind, which made him nervous and insecure. But forcing himself to fly and explore he finally found a forest abundant with trees and fruit. Here is the question. While dwelling in the barren tree, could you have convinced the sparrow of the existence of the forest?

55. Q: It seems we must disbelieve many things we once accepted as right and good.

A: Quite correct. For example, every man who has found the loftier life once decided to disbelieve society when it insisted it knew what was best for him.

56. Q: We make so many mistakes at the start of the journey. Please explain one of them.

A: People want to approach Truth on their own conditions, which is like demanding to enter a king's court dressed in rags. Truth will not accept our demands, but it will accept our authentic wish to change.

57. Q: What kind of demands must we drop?

A: One example would be the demand to always be in the right. People like to make a great public show of admitting their mistakes, but they secretly insist they are right. Truth asks us to concede that we are wrong. It asks this not to hurt us, but to help us become right.

58. Q: How have others succeeded?

A: One student helped his upward climb by asking himself, "Might I be distorting my own life without realizing it?"

59. Q: What is required of an individual?

A: A man needed a special kind of lantern for traveling at night. He called on several shops, but they stocked no such lantern. Discouraged, he finally entered a small shop in an obscure part of town. The shopkeeper explained,"This is such a special lantern it cannot be bought. Each person must make his own. However, I can teach you the skill. Are you interested in learning?"

60. Q: You say there is a great reason to be in good cheer. What is the reason?

A: There is something else.

CHAPTER 1 IN SUMMARY

a. Fear is a hoax which you can unmask right now.

b. Walk through the open door to life-command.

c. Esoteric ideas are the royal road to self-newness.

d. Refuse to be intimidated by negative thoughts.

e. Rely upon your own emerging cosmic powers.

f. See that these teachings are wonderfully sensible.

g. Willingness to learn is a great power for learning.

h. Dare to travel beyond ordinary thinking habits.

i. Any start along the path is a good start.

j. Remain cheerful, for there is a new world!

Chapter 2

MAKE SWIFT AND PLEASANT PROGRESS

61. Q: You recently commented that authentic sincerity was a power for real self-change. I appreciate that.

A: Fifty people were lost in the wilderness. But only one of them admitted he was lost. The others pretended they knew the way out, so they wandered and bluffed and suffered. But the admission of the fiftieth man gave his mind a special alertness. He finally noticed a faint trail which he followed out of the wilderness.

62. Q: I know that anxiety of any kind is wrong, but I am anxious to see results from my inner efforts.

A: Have you ever tried being patient with yourself—as patient as you like others to be with you? Patiently collect facts, patiently act upon them. Results will come.

63. Q: I want to break out of myself, but my failures and humiliation overwhelm me. What can I do?

A: Do what is necessary and forget everything else. Never mind any humiliation or pain or distress. Just do what is necessary in order to break out.

64. Q: I am not sure I know what is necessary.

A: The necessary always involves replacing mechanical behavior with conscious action. The problem is that mechanicalness never sees itself as mechanical, so it calls itself conscious. Mechanical people who believe they are conscious fight wars and commit crimes and spread general misery around the world. This class will help you distinguish between mechanical behavior and conscious action.

65. Q: Is conscious action the same as peaceful action?

A: Yes, because it is undivided. Mechanical action is divided against itself. Take motives. A man has two motives—the noble one he publicly claims to have and the hidden motive of adding to his vanity or to his bank account. So mechanicalness causes self-division, and self-division causes conflict.

66. Q: I now see these ideas as absolutely essential to me, but a few years ago they meant nothing. What was wrong with me?

A: The same thing that is wrong with everyone else. You were hiding—hiding from facts you wrongly assumed threatened your existence. How can you serve dinner to a hungry man who insists on hiding in the cellar?

67. Q: How can we increase the speed of our upward climb?

A: You must reach a certain level in your climbing. You must reach the point where you are willing to accept a bit of new knowledge while sensing it means the end of a particular conceit.

68. Q: So how can we see and end conceit?

A: Stop calling it something else. Stop covering the brutal chain with gold paint and calling it valuable jewelry.

69. Q: Stop calling mechanical religious activities a spiritual way of life?

A: And stop saying you are concerned for other people when you are really concerned with hearing public applause for your so-called concern.

70. Q: What do you mean by a jolting but healthy lesson?

A: Suppose you are discussing spiritual topics with someone. His words and facial expressions plainly reveal that he is fearfully fighting the facts he needs. You ask him, "Do you want wholeness or do you want to argue?" He will feel jolted because you have suddenly made him aware of his actual state of hostility. He must then choose whether to take the jolt as a healthy lesson in self-insight or to argue all the more.

71. Q: Unfortunately, most people choose to argue.

A: Because they are afraid. They fear letting go of what they have always called themselves. They do not see that there is no real danger in letting go. They do not realize that danger remains only because they do not let go.

25

72. Q: The weekly study group in my home town is doing nicely, but we need to arouse ourselves. May we have an exercise for seeing life clearly?

A: Spend an evening in defining the human condition from the higher viewpoint. For example, stupidity is unawareness of self and life.

73. Q: May we have more examples?

A: Stubbornness is ignorance masquerading as will-power. Evil is anything unconscious that should be conscious. Continued artificiality is the senseless fear of abandoning familiar and comfortable errors. Sarcastic criticism is a worthless substitute for understanding.

74. Q: We distort words to fit our vanities. With this in mind, what is authentic heroism?

A: Real heroism is the act of trying to stand alone while having no clear idea of what it means to stand alone.

75. Q: I have just seen how timid I am toward the truth. Sometimes I have strange feelings toward the new ideas given in this class.

A: A man in a dark cave for a long time feels strange when stepping out into the sunlight. You need never fear anything you hear in this class. Every idea is a spiritual vitamin. In time the strange will be seen as the friendly.

76. Q: Can anyone succeed in this?

A: Anyone loving rightness over reputation.

77. Q: How have other people succeeded?

A: Two students in a class were asked to give brief and helpful statements. One student said, "A book containing truthful principles is one of the greatest treasures on earth." The other student stated, "Every effort to awaken ourselves from psychic sleep will be rewarded, and the reward will be one less nightmare."

78. Q: So many exterior conditions seem to block the interior journey. How can we get them out of the way?

A: I will answer that by asking you two questions. Are you aware that you are standing in your own way? Are you trying to stop it?

79. Q: You say that our blunders are so gigantic we would be horrified to face them. Since the facing is necessary, please mention one of these gigantic blunders.

A: People deceive themselves into believing they are trusting God or Truth when they are really trusting their own egotism. This is because they mistake God for egotism. Such people are often ill-tempered and arrogant. They do not even trust God to make them pleasant people. They sense their self-deception, but need real humility to end it.

80. Q: I listen and study and apply, but am still attacked by fearful doubt.

A: You can attain a state of mind in which doubt is as absent as snow in summer. Truth cannot doubt itself. Become truth itself. You can succeed.

81. Q: Please supply a rule for steady progress.

A: A child living with his parents in the wilderness wanted to know how far he could safely wander. His father told him to keep the home in sight at all times. So explore the world of ideas, but keep these basic principles in sight at all times.

82. Q: What basic principle explains self-transformation?

A: Real change results from the dropping of something—a wrong attitude, an unseen resistance, a harmful emotion.

83. Q: Help us increase our cosmic daring.

A: Think of any great explorer in history, perhaps Columbus or Marco Polo. Imagine him saying, "I will venture into unknown worlds only if I know beforehand what they are like." In the first place it is impossible to know before you see. Also he could not say that and still be a daring explorer. And neither can we find new cosmic worlds by demanding to know their nature in advance. So make this truly daring declaration, "I will enter the adventure, letting Reality reveal its rightness in its own way."

84. Q: I have trusted dozens of different paths but none have led me anywhere worthwhile.

A: How strange that we trust everything but that which alone is worthy of trust—God, Truth, Reality.

85.   Q: You once remarked that a feeling of helplessness can be the start of a truly spiritual life, provided it knocks out self-conceit. That helped me in a curious way.

A: The spiritual road starts on a dry prairie where we feel lost and helpless. But walk forward. A year later, if you have sighted only one green tree you never saw before, you are doing great!

86.   Q: How far can I go with these studies?

A: As far as you want to go. But do not deceive yourself about your willingness to travel far. Unseen resistances are within. One requirement for traveling far is to undeceive ourselves about our imagined joy over the journey.

87.   Q: Please supply some facts about knowing ourselves.

A: Self-knowledge includes insight into how negative we really are. That is an important part of the cure. But self-knowledge also includes glimpses of what we can do for ourselves; of truly positive actions we can take. One superb action is to work with a fact until making it your personal possession. The fact then commands your life, but since it is your fact you are really commanding yourself. Here is a good fact to think about and act upon: "Regardless of how I presently think and feel, it can be done."

88.   Q: I think I am making progress. I see through society's active ignorance.

A: Confused human activity is like a walking man who does not know where he is going who suddenly decides to run.

89. Q: I want to seek the truth but have no idea of its nature.

A: May I make a correction? You do have an idea of the nature of truth but since it is unconscious you do not see it. But it is precisely this *idea* about truth that prevents the appearance of truth itself. In future classes we will see how ideas and thoughts and words form a thick wall between us and truth. We will also learn how to break down the wall.

90. Q: What determines our perseverance?

A: Your thirst for cosmic health. A thirsty eagle flying toward a lake remains in flight, paying no attention to critical parrots or strutting crows who prefer to remain on the ground.

91. Q: By parrots and crows do you mean people who prefer to remain under psychic hypnosis?

A: And who will unconsciously and maliciously try to ruin your flight. Egotism has no conscience whatever. It wants everyone else to remain as miserable as it is.

92. Q: What do these teachings mean when saying that we must rise above the level of words?

A: A part of you can understand truth without using words, just as you can silently understand a beautiful grove.

93. Q: Please give us something to understand silently.

A: Rising above oneself, which is a great spiritual miracle, consists of letting self-knowledge reveal that one is not the imaginary self he had taken himself to be all these years.

94. Q: How can we work earnestly at self-transformation, instead of merely playing games?

A: We do real spiritual work when seeing its necessity, and a single honest glance at our actual condition will reveal the necessity.

95. Q: I like the idea of using everything for progress.

A: A seeker wished to ascend to a Temple of Truth which stood on a hill before him. But there were no upward steps, rather, the hillside was covered with rocks. He finally understood what other seekers before him had perceived. Rightly used, the rocks themselves became upward steps. One marvel of the path is the way in which obstacles and hurts and bewilderments can be used for progress.

96. Q: When will we really be on the way?

A: When you don't know where you are going but know you must go.

97. Q: I always wonder whether I can take the next step.

A: Take it. I will show you where you are

going wrong. You are not concerned with the next step, but with idle thoughts about the success or failure of the next step. Stop wasting mental energy. Take the next step, large or small, with no concern for results. Do this and the next step will reveal itself to you every time.

98.　Q: I have acquired many new ideas, but remain the same bewildered person I was before.
　　　A: New ideas can change the direction of your walk, but they are not the complete journey. The advanced journey consists of seeing oneself in a totally different way, for example, seeing the emptiness of public applause. Still, the advanced journey becomes possible with new ideas.

99.　Q: Help us make the most of small gains.
　　　A: When noticing your inner progress, realize that it is only a small part of what you can do for yourself. This prevents limiting walls from rising.

100.　Q: Someone remarked that we go where truth goes or we go nowhere. That means truth never compromisies.
　　　A: It is as impossible for truth to compromise as it is for water to become rocks.

101.　Q: I doubt that many people see this.
　　　A: Any attempt to popularize truth will fail, for truth will not compromise in order to be accepted by masses of people. Truth does not

mingle with huge crowds and has no part in religious propaganda. Truth may appear to be present in popular religious and social movements, but only to those who want syrup instead of healing medicine.

102. Q: I try to learn these lessons but always feel as if I am about to be expelled for stupidity.

A: Wisdom does not expel anyone. That is not its nature. You can be expelled only by your own conceit or some other foolishness. Love wisdom more than conceit and you will progress nicely in the cosmic college.

103. Q: How do we limit our cosmic comprehension?

A: A bird walking along the seashore cannot see the immensity of the ocean. It is not understood by him even when told about it by others who know. But when taking flight he begins to see the vastness for himself. Start your cosmic flight by declining to accept your present view as the only view.

104. Q: Help us to think logically toward inner success.

A: Think of three steps—information, action, transformation. First you collect higher facts. Then you apply them to daily experiences, such as taking an ego-defeat consciously instead of with mechanical anxiety. This leads to a profound change in your very nature, which may start with the new feeling that you are not permanently chained to secret despair.

105. Q: We are frozen by fear of making mistakes.

A: You hesitate to climb the cosmic mountain for fear of making mistakes? Give yourself permission to make ten thousand mistakes, all the mistakes necessary to reach the peak.

106. Q: How can I tell whether or not I am advancing toward true life?

A: One sign is a changing attitude toward unfolding events. Less and less do we demand that events conform to our insistent cravings. This indicates a falling away of a particular false belief— the belief that we possess separate selves which can and must control events. The realization of Oneness is coming closer, as is psychic maturity and authentic contentment.

107. Q: I am trying to walk the path, but everything seems to stand in my way.

A: I don't accept that conclusion for you at all. Anyone who feels that everything stands in his way can use these facts to see that nothing stands in his way.

108. Q: How might we be proceeding incorrectly?

A: For many years a man tried to bring peace into his exterior conditions. He finally succeeded by bringing peace into his interior conditions.

109. Q: Over and over I have wrestled with the problem of admitting only right ideas into my mind. I am not sure I know a right idea when it appears.

A: Truth knows. Become truth. You can do it. Then you will know. Truth is a wise shepherd who admits only innocent lambs into the meadow, such as diligence and earnestness. It denies entrance to negative creatures such as scorn and sullenness.

110. Q: I have a major problem. Sometimes I wander off the path because I feel unworthy, sometimes because I am weak, and for a dozen other reasons.

A: There is no problem at all. Why do you make one? Continue to walk the path in spite of everything. That is all there is to it. See how simply the problem is solved?

111. Q: Everyone gives me different and often contradictory advice. Who is telling the truth—if any of them?

A: Your own real nature knows the difference between true advice and nonsensical babble, so awaken this natural intelligence through inner exploration.

112. Q: In what way does cosmic law help us?

A: As a lamb attracts its mother, a little truth in spiritual matters attracts larger truth.

113. Q: Why do we fail to learn our spiritual lessons?

A: Most human beings cannot even take the first lesson in becoming whole. Do you know what this highly objectionable first lesson is? It is to tell a man or woman, "There is something seriously wrong with you." Do you think their fear and vanity wants to hear that? Never. But those who sincerely examine the fact will change the fact.

114. Q: Give us a guide for true action.

A: What society seeks, ignore. What society ignores, seek.

115. Q: The daily battle is exhausting. What can we do?

A: You can learn to stop fighting. Man is like a soldier who fights the same battle over every day, sometimes winning, sometimes losing, but forever forced to fight. He knows the battlefield, knows the faces of the enemy, but never knows how to end the exhausting conflict.

116. Q: How can we do something right for ourselves?

A: Make the unseen seen. Suppose a man attends a meeting where truth is actually presented. Perhaps he hears ten things he does not want to hear. He will not even be aware of his resistance to what he needs. So what is right for him? He must see how he is presently doing something against himself. Awareness of resistance erases it.

117. Q: So it is what we don't see that hurts us?

A: An explorer in Africa wished to reach

Victoria Falls. He was opposed by troubles, including the mysterious disappearance of supplies. He believed that surrounding tribes were against him, when in fact he was being betrayed by members of his own party. Inwardly, we have unseen resistances to truth, which must be exposed and banished.

118. Q: Give us something to work with for the rest of the day.

A: Understand that a simple fact has extraordinary power to change a receptive mind.

119. Q: Please give us one such fact.

A. Be right by being willing to be wrong.

120. Q: These teachings seem to ask us to do so many things we don't want to do!

A: What parts of you don't want to do them? I will tell you. The timid and lazy parts, the parts that want to keep you enslaved. And you go along with *them?* Does a prisoner agree with his jailer? Break out!

121. Q: The false part of us shakes when hearing the truth, and wants to run away. How can it be defeated?

A: Stand and shake. Stand and shake. Stand and shake. But *stand.*

A REVIEW OF HELPFUL POINTS

a. Patient effort delivers beneficial results.

b. Use jolts from life as healthy cosmic lessons.

c. An effort to stand alone is authentic heroism.

d. True ideas seem strange when first hearing them.

e. A love for rightness attracts more rightness.

f. You can go as far as you really want to go!

g. Self-knowledge creates inner miracles.

h. Truth never rejects a slow but sincere pupil.

i. Continue to walk the path in spite of everything.

j. These ideas help you to do good for yourself.

Chapter 3

TAKE COMMAND IN HUMAN RELATIONS

122. Q: People expect so much of me, but I cannot live up to what they wish.

A: You are not required to live up to what others expect you to be, but only to what your real nature invites you to be.

123. Q: That is as refreshing as a stream in the desert.

A: You will constantly meet such refreshing truths as you proceed with the inner adventure.

124. Q: Can human quarrels come to an end?

A: Imagine some primitive men arguing and fighting over the best way to row their crude boats. Then one day they discover the principle of sailing with the power of the wind. All arguments cease. Men will cease quarreling over religion, social matters, and everything else once they discover the superior power of Cosmic Mind.

125. Q: Why do so many male and female relation-ships start off with moonlight and roses but end with a storm?

A: Because you do not see people as they really are but through the fog of your own ideas about them. And your own ideas will always connect in some way with your own false idolization of others. You think that woman is nice?

Your insecurity paints a beautiful but hazardous picture of her so that you might feel loved and needed. You believe that man is strong? It is because your own weakness wants someone to lean on.

126. Q: I have had enough bitter experiences with people to see the truth of that. Sooner or later—the wakening shock. I have had enough of playing the nervous game.

A: That is what attracted you to this class. You are weary of the deceptive game. Congratulations.

127. Q: Please explain the cause and the cure for feeling burdened by other people.

A: It is impossible for anyone to be burdened by others unless he is first a burden to himself, for both burdens are boulders from the same inner ground.

128. Q: Why does the world go as it goes?

A: World events happen because of far different causes than imagined. You may think they happen because of conscious human choices and intelligent planning and hopes for a better life for all. They happen in fact because of human hypnosis and subtle cruelty and self-destructive tendencies.

129. Q: What psychic law should we understand to make us more competent in human relations?

A: It is psychic law that a person either helps or hurts other people to the exact degree that he helps or hurts himself. This law is not seen by those who wish to keep hurting themselves and others.

130. Q: I fear that people and events can hurt me.

A: No one is really trying to break into your psychic home to scare and hurt you. Just make an effort to awaken from the dreadful nightmare. We will help you in this class. You can awaken to a calm understanding that all is well.

131. Q: What wise guide might we use when meeting new people?

A: New people in your life will treat you the way they are internally, so make it your wise business to see them as they really are.

132. Q: And we can develop this ability?

A: If you want the ability more than you want to remain with your habitual ways.

133. Q: It is encouraging to know that it can be done.

A: A wise man had an unusual ability to see through the artificiality of human behavior. One day his friends asked him to comment on several passers-by. The wise man stated, "That man is pretending to know what he does not know. And that man is pretending to be respectful to others. And that man—heaven help him—is pretending that he is not pretending."

134. Q: I try to help someone who is determined to ruin his life. My pain and frustration are dreadful.

A: I want you to deeply realize that every human being is responsible for his own behavior. This will make you right, regardless of his destructive ways. Then, your rightness is true love, for love understands everything about the human condition here on earth.

135. Q: I am getting well-acquainted with a certain person. Can this familiarity create love?

A: No. Familiarity merely lessens certain tensions at the start, then can easily slide into contempt. A deceitful person reveals scorn toward those he has used to satisfy his own neurotic needs. Your own experiences with people prove this. Love is not on that level.

136. Q: I don't understand what it means to choose in favor of what is right for me.

A: Truth does not take pleasure in your downfall. Your so called friends take secret pleasure in your calamity. Which do you choose for companionship?

137. Q: But don't we need friends?

A: You need relationship. What is its quality? The quality will rise as you uplift your own consciousness. High quality consciousness creates your own right relationship with everyone. This simply means you know how to act wisely toward both cruel and pleasant people.

138. Q: More and more I see that a deep knowledge of human nature offers solid protection in society. May we have an example of this protective knowledge?

A: People who have injured their own lives will not hesitate to injure your life. It can be done very cunningly, often under the guise of goodness. Self-injury and other-injury occupy the same psychic level.

139. Q: We don't see people as they are?

A: You never see people as they are. You see skilled and charming actors and actresses so self-hypnotized by their roles that they believe they are real, which hypnotizes you into believing they are real.

140. Q: Years ago I would never have accepted that. I would have thought it harsh and unkind.

A: It is harsh and unkind to not see people as they are, for that perpetuates all the illusions responsible for human hypocrisy and cruelty. An individual's only chance is to face the facts about himself and others, for a faced fact can be changed.

141. Q: Please supply more insight into human nature.

A: People who say they are sorry will do it again. Their sorriness is a combination of shame and a regret at having lost former advantages. Their basic nature remains unchanged, so they must repeat their negative behavior. There is a different kind of sorriness which includes insight into self-destructive behavior. This can change a person.

142. Q: Why do human beings neglect higher life?

A: One feature of the unconscious man who believes he is conscious is that *he never knows what he is missing.* And he cannot possibly know as long as delusion is his darling. Talking to him about higher life is like telling a sheep about stars. Only a cosmically mature mind can comprehend lofty levels.

143. Q: Maybe I'm the suggestible type but I easily fall under the influence of people who urge me to adopt their religious beliefs or their social practices. I find it hard to say no.

A: Remember what I am about to tell you and it will be easy to say no. When people urge you to live as they do they are really inviting you to be as miserable as they are.

144. Q: I cannot understand how a person can switch so often from goodness to badness and back to goodness again. What is my mistake?

A: You think a man is bad only when he expresses it outwardly, perhaps in cruelty against you. Later, when he has quieted down you think he has switched over to goodness. Nothing of the sort. His badness is simply dozing for awhile. Does a sleeping tiger turn into a lamb? Let this bit of knowledge contribute to your freedom from the tiger.

44

145. Q: A friend has the habit of blaming everything but his own negative nature for his misfortunes. What might I tell him?

A: If you insist upon living in an internal zoo you must expect bites and scratches.

146. Q: Suppose a large audience is given the facts by which the listeners could rescue themselves. Can their secret reactions be seen and predicted?

A: Their behavior can be predicted precisely. Each will fight the facts, unaware of doing so. Each will fight in a different way—with childish arguing, with intellectual theories, with sarcasm loaded with fear, with artificial smiles of agreement, with boredom, with questions intended to embarrass the speaker, and so on. Each will have to return home to continue to live with a miserable and unwanted self.

147. Q: But this seems so hard on people. Don't most men and women want the rescuing facts?

A: What do you really think?

148. Q: I am afraid of a certain angry person.

A: The fear exists only in your own mind. However, you do not see this as yet, for you wrongly attribute power to this person. Recover your own power of pure thought. Do you know what you will then see? You will see that you were fearing a frightened and angry sheep.

149. Q: Are you saying we can break our psychic chains by daring to doubt society's foolish values?

A: Which means you can no longer desire society's foolish rewards.

150. Q: What kind of rewards?

A: Do you wish public honors and bank accounts or do you wish to stop being a self-divided human being?

151. Q: As a practical project you instructed us to observe a particular trait in people. I was astonished at what I saw clearly for the first time. Everyone is so touchy, self-defensive.

A: Then be glad you are here in class. Truth offers a rich gift to those who feel they must constantly and angrily defend themselves. The gift is freedom from painful and fearful self-defense.

152. Q: How is this accomplished?

A: By realizing that self-defense is really the defense of a fictitious person. This fact is startling to people when hearing it for the first time; they simply cannot accept it. Nevertheless, each time we defend this imaginary person we strengthen the illusion that it is real. So no self-defense weakens and finally ends this troublemaker.

153. Q: When will I feel free from domineering people?

A: When will you stop explaining yourself to people who insist you owe them an explanation?

154. Q: After much digging I have discovered a major fear of most of us—the fear of rejection. What about it?

A: You have made a valuable discovery. People will do almost anything to avoid feeling rejected. They know that rejection causes a surge of fear of not knowing who they are. But who is being rejected? Your acquired ideas about yourself and nothing else. Practice conscious rejection, which means you will understand that your ideas about yourself may be rejected, but that you are not these ideas.

155. Q: I am bothered by people who do not think well of me, by those who criticize and disapprove.

A: No. You are not really bothered by what others think of you. You are bothered by what you think of yourself.

156. Q: Criticism makes me think less of myself?

A: It shakes the imaginations you have about yourself. You have complimentary and unconscious images of yourself as being honest or pleasant or competent or whatever. Criticism disturbs these images, making you unsure of who you are. This makes you nervous and irritable. Get rid of your self-images and you will not be bothered by criticism, for then you will really know who you are.

157. Q: But who am I?

A: You know that when you don't think about it.

158.   Q: I feel painfully left out of things.

A: The next time society leaves you out of something, be glad you don't have to frantically fight your way out of what you might have foolishly walked into.

159.   Q: Recently I had a small but helpful jolt. I saw that friendship is not what society claims it to be.

A: Your only real friends are those men and women who want to find themselves. All else is shallow association without value. There was once a country in which truth and decency were scorned, while hypocrisy and treachery were practiced as a way of life. But there was also a small group of truth-seekers in the country. They were real friends, for they gave and received only the guiding light.

160.   Q: I have met a few people who said they were free from all anger. Please comment.

A: There was once a very angry man. One day he took his anger to a nearby animal's cave and hid it inside. "There!" he exclaimed, "I have rid myself of anger!" He repeated this idea so often he finallly believed his own lie. The man suffered terribly from anger, for it emerged often from the cave to attack him. He had not freed himself from anger, but had merely hidden it from sight.

161. Q: But is freedom from anger really possible?

A: Of course it is. It will happen when you no longer have unconscious assumptions about who you are.

162. Q: Please make that clearer.

A: When you have the idea that you are a non-angry person you are simply an angry person calling yourself non-angry because it seems to supply certain rewards. When through self-insight you no longer call yourself either angry or non-angry you have risen above the level of ideas, of thoughts. On that higher level, that conscious level, there is no anger.

163. Q: There is an abundance of religious and philosophical activity in the world, but truly nice people are still hard to find.

A: A truly nice person is someone who has really found himself.

164. Q: So why are such people seldom seen?

A: For every man who wants to find himself there are a million men who want to *say* they want to find themselves.

165. Q: All the great teachers state that few people really want to find the way out. How true.

A: Let those who want to play games play games. You have something to make of your life here on earth, something far greater than making others take notice of you.

166. Q: For a long time I considered myself an expert in knowing human nature, but my conflicts with people say something else. What am I failing to see?

A: Many things, but I will select one of them. You fail to see the other person as a totally confused human being. You fail to see the man behind the many masks. It is his swift and unexpected change of masks that hurts and bewilders you. He or she is friendly one minute and tricky the next.

167. Q: You explained it perfectly. Why does this error persist?

A: For two reasons. First, you do not see the same total confusion in yourself, so cannot detect it in others. It is psychic law that ignorance of oneself must project itself outwardly into ignorance of others. You do not really see the other person; you see your own distorted views about him.

168. Q: The other reason?

A: Lack of self-reliance. You hope the other person is stronger, wiser, more capable and more loving than you are. This supplies a false sense of security which must crumble sooner or later. Why not be your own strength?

169. Q: I don't know how to handle destructive behavior in either myself or others.

A: You can wisely use darkness in other

people to end darkness in yourself. Evil is very stupid; it shows you exactly how it can be destroyed. Suppose you observe someone in a hateful mood. With a little insight you can also observe how that person torments himself with his own hatred. Now, do you really want to torment *yourself* with dark emotions? Of course not. This insight has already broken a small chain.

170. Q: This is effective because we can see others clearer than we see ourselves?

A: That is part of it. General effectiveness depends upon the strength of your wish to drop inner chains.

171. Q: Society is dedicated to making society sick.

A: One thousand people started to climb the spiritual mountain. They came to the place where unconscious pretense had to be abandoned before proceeding upward. Nine hundred and ninety-nine stopped climbing.

172. Q: Why is it so difficult to attain a state of real decency, or even admit its existence?

A: Can a pouncing hawk know the peaceful nature of a dove? Never. The hawk can see only what he is—a pouncing hawk. He will therefore scorn the very idea of a nature different from his own.

173. Q: Then what chance does anyone have of becoming a dove?

A: Everyone has a great chance. It starts when the hawk no longer pretends he is already a dove. That is the hawk's main problem—he falsely labels himself a dove.

174. Q: I am puzzled by our refusal to examine our lives. It is obvious that we are heading in the wrong direction, still we refuse to look at where we are going.

A: People will not look at where they are going for fear of discovering they are going nowhere, which they are. Honest self-examination is the only way to create a cosmic compass.

175. Q: But how many people will do this?
A: Will you do it?

176. Q: How do people unconsciously avoid self-facing?

A: The more a man neglects his own life the more he will be compelled to wrongly involve himself in the lives of others. This accounts for the neurotic reformer, the busybody, the general troublemaker. Being self-deceived he will always credit himself with noble motives. This is a good example of the wrong use of natural energy.

177. Q: I am afraid we rarely see ourselves as others see us.

A: Ah, yes. The more obnoxious the man the more he is sure that others cannot survive without his charming company.

178. Q: I want to escape but don't even know what I must escape from.

A: Make the smallest attempt to escape the human trap and guilty people will try to make you feel guilty about it. Escape from them. Don't listen to them. Start to purify your own mental stream by not permitting people to toss their incredible nonsense into it.

179. Q: Self-correction corrects outer areas. Where can we start?

A: Begin to suspect that you may be doing many unnecessary things in your day. For example, you may be wasting yourself in trying to please demanding people who are incapable of being pleased.

180. Q: That hits home. Please add to it.

A: Vow that you will never again please anyone so that he or she will be pleased with you. Succeed in this and you will hear another chain drop.

181. Q: I see the logic of it. We often please people because we fear to lose their favors. This fear cannot be right.

A: Conscious love has no fear.

182. Q: I see so much bitterness in people, perhaps in myself. What is the cause and cure?

A: Bitterness is the outcome of a wrong mental movement—the attempt to force external

53

events to conform to internal fantasy. The cure is to see fantasy as fantasy, which will reveal it as neither necessary nor rewarding.

183. Q: What is an example of a self-punishing condition?

A: Outer dignity, inner disorder.

184. Q: We feel a thrill when winning over other people, when gaining an advantage over them. There is something wrong with this kind of a thrill. What is it?

A: Any so-called victory over other people must be paid for with the fear that they will next win over you. Study this psychic law until you end the desire for such thrills.

185. Q: I have always feared ridicule. It has forced me into foolish compromise and conformity.

A: Fearing that other people may laugh at you is simply another misunderstanding which self-knowledge can erase.

186. Q: I have had some difficulties with relatives. I don't know how to talk to them to solve the problem.

A: Never mind solving the problem. Solve yourself. You are the only problem you have. Look deeply until you see. The seeing and the solving are the same thing.

187. Q: What determines the result of a new human relationship?

A: The outcome of every human contact for either harmony or heartache is decided by the kind of nature you actually possess and the kind of nature actually possessed by the other person. In these few words you have a cosmic college course in human relations.

SPECIAL IDEAS IN THIS CHAPTER

a. See people as they are, not as they appear.

b. If you want out of the social trap—congratulations!

c. Cosmic consciousness is the same as authentic love.

d. You cannot talk to a sheep about stars.

e. Your real nature never fears another human being.

f. It is not your duty to explain yourself to others.

g. These truths banish anxiety over being rejected.

h. Your real friends are people who wish cosmic facts.

i. Insight into human nature protects you from people.

j. Self-facing is honest and healthy and miraculous.

Chapter 4

HOW TO WIN HIGHER GUIDANCE

188. Q: How can we recognize and remain on the right path?

A: Imagine yourself hiking a forest trail with the aim of reaching the peak of a distant mountain. Coming to many forks along the trail, you don't know which way to turn. This is not a severe problem as long as you maintain your wish for the mountain. See why? Your clear goal enables you to recognize the wrong path, for you see how it takes you away from the mountain, not toward it. Loyalty to your lofty aim is your corrective guide.

189. Q: Too often we do not know where to look for answers.

A: To understand where you must *not* look for answers is superb progress in itself. This means you must attain healthy disillusionment. Start by being disillusioned with glittering but empty social schemes for human betterment.

190. Q: How can we experience higher power?

A: You are not condemned for anything but you are also not excused from anything. See these two ideas together at the same time and a powerful third force for self-awakening is created.

191. Q: Why do we fail to understand answers to our questions?

A: The true answer to a question resides on a higher level than the question. Therefore a sincere person asking a question should not expect the answer to be immediately clear to him. He should not be discouraged by his lack of comprehension, but should patiently lift his consciousness up to the level of the answer. When an insincere person hears a true answer he gains nothing, for he instantly and fearfully distorts it to fit his own egotistical illusions.

192. Q: We need help from those who really know the answers, but must retain mental independence. Please comment.

A: At the start we need others to remind us of what we must do, but eventually we remind ourselves, like having an internal guidebook which can be read instantly by our spiritual eyes.

193. Q: How can we contact right guidance?

A: Truth invites. Its invitation is always open. Anyone can accept the invitation any time. But understand something quite clearly. Truth invites—and then stops. It stops because it knows the individual must make the next move. Truth never pleads or compromises or wavers. It invites and awaits your acceptance.

194. Q: I feel like someone trapped in a big and brawling city. I feel helpless, ignorant of what to do.

A: You may not realize it as yet but you can

57

always go home. You can always do that. Then you will know what to do, just as you know how to handle the stove and refrigerator in your physical house. You cannot know what to do while remaining in the noisy city, for you are still part of its confusion.

195. Q: By going home I think you mean we must return to our real nature.

A: That is one way to say it. But let's emphasize a particular point. In order to reach home where you have the guidance of cosmic insight you must first depart from your present location. You cannot remain in the noisy city of your own vanities and expect to know what to do. Cosmic knowledge and personal vanity do not mingle.

196. Q: So going home means to deliberately depart from everything wrong within ourselves.

A: Exactly. So do it. First you will catch a faint glimpse of your restful residence, and then you will be one with it.

197. Q: Where are we overlooking right help?

A: A new employee at a mountain resort was instructed to repair a sign which stood on top of a hill. He was about to start the long upward hike when he was told, "Take that electric car over there. That is what it is for." Cosmic knowledge works for you. That is what it is for. Take it.

198. Q: Guide us toward intelligent action.

A: It is the highest form of active intelligence to let whatever is right within grow at the expense of whatever is wrong.

199. Q: Please identify a common wrongness.

A: No longer waste thoughts over what others think of you, instead, think how you can be free of all such worthless thoughts.

200. Q: Life piles on the difficulties of frustrated plans, ill health, domestic quarrels. I never know which way to turn.

A: Whatever the difficulty there is only one way to turn. Turn to study. Study your mind, study surrounding life, study human nature, study cosmic ideas. This is turning toward the Supreme Source of Solutions. This is rejected by the self-deceived who trust in social solutions. But it is perfect guidance and great relief to those who have caught a glimpse of something higher than themselves.

201. Q: Where should we be cautious when seeking help?

A: Never permit a defeated person to convince you that he can help you win inner victory, for he is simply exploiting you to maintain his own delusion of being a victor.

202. Q: Where might we make a mistake when consulting someone who really knows the answers?

A: When requesting help from an authentic teacher we must not try to impose our stale ideas upon him, for that would be like the patient telling the doctor what to do.

203. Q: Sometimes I feel I am on a collision course that nothing can stop.

A: It can be stopped. Something higher than your usual self can stop it. But I must ask you a question. What false condition are you willing to sacrifice in order to find this higher power?

204. Q: So much is asked!

A: So much is given.

205. Q: Our illogic causes our ills.

A: Then develop two kinds of logic. One can be called everyday logic. It keeps your day running smoothly. You use everyday logic when shopping wisely or driving safely. Spiritual logic consists of understanding and living within cosmic laws. With it you know what life is all about and have self-independence. Strong spiritual logic can build stronger everyday logic.

206. Q: What bars us from developing higher logic?

A: The assumption that we already have it. Remember, illogic never sees itself, as with the man who asked indignantly, "Why didn't you say so before you spoke?"

207. Q: Please comment on the need for going beyond spiritual knowledge.

A: The acquisition of spiritual facts is necessary, but it is only the first section of the upward path. This section ends at the edge of a cliff. To continue to climb we must bravely leap over to the opposite cliff where essence becomes alive. The leap is made by dropping vanity over knowledge and by a willingness to become nothing in order to become everything.

208. Q: It seems that a misuse of imagination causes far more grief than we think.

A: Especially when people imagine they have found a source of true guidance. You can observe this everywhere in society. A group of people huddle fearfully together in a swamp, agreeing to deceive each other by calling it a meadow. It is still a swamp, and something within every man and woman knows it.

209. Q: Can they escape?

A: Yes, if they are willing to do what is necessary. It is necessary at the start for a man to see how fearful and angry he becomes when his false position is questioned. Never forget that anyone in a false position will become hostile when truth touches his pretense, though he may conceal his malice by a forced exterior calmness. His very hostility proves his weakness, but he must see and admit it personally.

210. Q: So the first step out of the swamp is to admit that we are in fact in the swamp.

A: Correct, but let me state it a bit differently. A man must come to the point in his life where he can no longer endure the painful deception of imagining that the swamp is a meadow. He is now in both the great crisis and the great opportunity of his life. He can choose the false security of remaining with the lost and stumbling group in the swamp or he can courageously choose to work his way out.

211. Q: We want out, but have so little courage.

A: I will see whether you really want out. If you do, courage will come of itself.

212. Q: What does it mean to give up something in order to win something else of a higher nature?

A: A rich but unhappy man sought help from a real teacher. "I will give up much of my wealth to find peace," promised the man. Replied the teacher, "No, no. That is too easy. Give up your vanity." Said the visitor, "I will also give up my public prominence." The teacher said, "No, no. That is too easy. Give up your pride over giving up so much."

213. Q: Many people would like to seek this new world but fear the absence of guidance.

A: Dare to start the search for the inner kingdom and instant guidance will appear, like seeing roadside signs pointing toward a distant castle.

214. Q: How can we receive something higher and better?

A: Uplift your wish, for wishes are answered according to their own level of quality or non-quality.

215. Q: May we hear more about the upward path?

A: Do you remember the first time you really did something about your life? Perhaps you bought your first book of cosmic facts or attended your first truth-class or wrote your first letter seeking information about higher studies. There will be many more first times, each one a bit higher than the one before. For the first time you will see how heartache can be used to end heartache, that self-release is not a terror but a victory.

216. Q: With right inner work we will eventually hear something that is not of our usual nature?

A: Correct. The need to follow the first faint whisperings of truth is illustrated by an explorer's experience. Lost in the jungle, he wandered helplessly for days. Then a faint and different kind of sound filtered through the trees. He followed the sound all the way to its source—a magnificent waterfall, a tourist attraction, where he received help.

217. Q: I don't know how to grasp these ideas.

A: Choose to grasp them. Persistent choice toward rightness generates power for perception.

Remember that cosmic fact and mental myth cannot occupy the same place at the same time, any more than two hands can occupy the same glove. So choose what is truly right for you.

218. Q: As hard as I try to convince myself that I know what it is all about, doubt creeps in to spoil my daydream.

A: Then stop involving yourself with things that must pile doubt upon doubt, and turn to celestial matters about which there is no doubt.

219. Q: Is there really a way to uplift human behavior?

A: There is no way to behave higher than the level of cosmic insight allows, but there is a way to raise the level of insight and therefore a way to uplift right behavior.

220. Q: Please describe this way.

A: Through inner effort one must first arrive at the place where he is capable of learning something new, like someone who willingly walks through the rain to reach a library.

221. Q: What do you mean by authentic help?

A: Society can only make an awkward and unsatisfactory attempt to help anyone out of trouble. The authentic help of these teachings shows him how to stay out of trouble in the first place.

222. Q: Why do we live as we do?

A: Everyone lives as he does because of the hourly choices he makes. Life-change becomes possible by changing the choices. For example, do you choose to understand a difficult situation or do you choose to fight it? Fighting prevents understanding. Choose to understand. That invites royal guidance.

223. Q: I like the idea of royal guidance.

A: A cosmic fact is like a king's messenger who arrives at the right time and place with perfect instructions.

224. Q: Give us something to build receptivity.

A: If told we are not yet capable of understanding something it is not an insult to our intelligence but a helpful step toward eventual understanding.

225. Q: Please speak about daily inner action.

A: Suppose each morning you sail the sea in a different kind of boat. One morning you roam around in a small motorboat, the next day on a yacht, and the third day in a rowboat. Daily spiritual work is like that. One day might be spent in reading, the next day in alert watchfulness of thoughts and feelings, the next day you take part in a group discussion. But all methods increase self-insight.

226. Q: Why does truth attract us?

A: Whether presently realized or not, there is something in you which is *not of your usual nature*. It is this unique nature which responds with interest to various truths in this class, which makes you feel something entirely different. You are like a botanist seeking a healthful herb in the forest. Catching your first faint fragrance of the herb, you know you are heading toward it.

227. Q: Misleading advice has been heaped upon my head since childhood. I can't afford any more of it.

A: Never listen to the advice of anyone who does not repeat the advice, "Look at yourself, work on yourself, rescue yourself."

228. Q: What are our sources of learning?

A: Learn from books and experiences, but above all learn from mental silence.

229. Q: The principle of self-guidance appeals to me, but seems so difficult and mysterious.

A: Only because you have not seriously tried it. Accurate self-guidance is as close as your own hand. Take a time when you feel bored. See that boredom exists only because your psychic system is operating incorrectly. That right first step in self-guidance can lead to additional help. Have a confident attitude toward self-guidance. That is important.

230. Q: A man is urged to counsel himself, but

look at where self-counsel has dragged him!

A: Up to now you have listened to counsel from what you have called your self, which is not you at all, but a bundle of mechanical habits. See this clearly, after which you will catch your first glimpse of the new nature within. This new nature is cosmic consciousness, which counsels you perfectly.

231. Q: You have made one thing clear. Our problem is in thinking we can do without spiritual wisdom.

A: If you can control a kite without a string, you can control your life without spiritual knowledge.

232. Q: I doubt my own answers, which is frightening.

A: It should be one of the most encouraging events of your life. It is wonderful to no longer have the kind of answers which have hurt you over the years. Be glad that your doubts are trying to teach you something new.

233. Q: How do we use spiritual facts wrongly?

A: A man was told about a buried treasure. He obtained a shovel. But being a foolish man he did an incredible thing. Instead of digging up the treasure he ran around boasting to everyone about his shovel! This is the unhappy state of those who preach spiritual facts while mistaking them for inner wealth. The treasure is found only when the false self yields to spiritual facts, as when one desires something higher than himself.

234. Q: We dimly realize the existence of something much higher, but we fear to let go of our earthly toys.

A: In the spiritual quest it is quite usual to fear the loss of things we consider valuable, but at a later stage we see their emptiness, and want nothing more than to lose them.

235. Q: We need to awaken to true values. How?

A: By remembering the single sentence I will now give you. All can go well outside, but if it is not going well inside, what is the outside worth?

236. Q: You once said we would win a new sense of rightness. You were right. I have attended these classes for only a short time, but already I sense the rightness in being here.

A: Association with right ideas is essential. You catch the falling apples by remaining in the orchard.

237. Q: I have plenty of work to do on myself, so I don't claim to be a teacher of others. But what can help me to help people who ask me about these higher facts?

A: Never forget the utter terror that people have for the truth that could set them free. You may think it an exaggeration when I tell you that people fear truth above all else. It is not exaggeration. The slightest hint to a man that he is not the separate self he believes he is will make him terrified and rageful. People are so accustomed to prison life that they take the cell as liberty and open field as the cell. Remembrance of this will help you help others—and yourself.

238.   Q: The world's surrounding evil is terrifying.

A: An evil merchant in ancient Arabia wanted to threaten and terrify a competitor. He wrote a vicious note prophesying doom for the other man, and gave it to a servant for delivery. But the servant returned with the note, explaining, "There was no one home to receive it." The evil of the world cannot reach anyone who is not home to it, whose spiritual level is above evil.

239.   Q: Why is rightness so remote?

A: Trying to get rightness from a self-centered mind is like trying to get perfume from a brick.

240.   Q: I wonder whether others have the same strange timidity that I sometimes have. I hesitate to submit to new ideas for fear they may rob me of my usual intelligence.

A: This is a common fear, especially with beginners. Submission to truth does not mean to abandon our intelligence, as we falsely fear. It means to drop that familiar but self-punishing train of thoughts we wrongly *call* intelligence. Go beyond this mere label and you will find Cosmic Intelligence.

241. Q: We are told to surrender ourselves to God, to Reality. I am not sure what this means.

A: Right surrender is to voluntarily detect and abandon everything inside you that causes trouble. Can you think of a happier task?

242. Q: So both the problem and the solution are within?

A: Like handing a block of pine to a skilled wood carver, give yourself over to that right part of you that really knows how to create something new, for it does exist within you.

243. Q: Where do we fail to understand cosmic law?

A: A foolish man observed a breeze and declared, "How nice it would be to make that breeze my own." So placing a bucket toward the breeze he tried to capture it. Failure made him bitter and resentful. He felt betrayed by nature. Foolish? No more foolish than those who believe it is both good and possible to capture life for their exclusive possession.

244. Q: I have understood these higher facts for a long time, but nothing seems to happen.

A: Try to understand a fact with your feelings as well as with your mind. For instance, try to feel the fact that the physical world you inhabit is not the only world.

245. Q: Then right feelings can help us?

A: In a fascinating way. Once you feel the difference between constructive forces and destructive forces, you begin to attract the constructive.

246. Q: Many of us knock on the door but remain outside.

A: Because knocking and entering are entirely different actions. Knocking is necessary, consisting of reading books, attending meetings, asking questions. But entrance requires much bolder action. It requires one to enter into himself, to uncover hidden motives, to see contradictions, and to realize his actual power for self-change.

247. Q: We need a reliable compass.

A: Certainly. That is why you are urged to collect pieces of knowledge. Collect the items needed to make a compass and truth will show you how to build it.

248. Q: I now have a fondness for some of the lessons which once appeared very severe. That is my personal miracle.

A: Imagine yourself driving a long highway leading from a low desert to a lofty mountain. You stop at various places along the way for a drink of water. You discover that the higher you go the purer the water becomes. Lessons about life are like that. As we drive upward they become more meaningful, more helpful.

BASIC FACTS FOR DAILY GUIDANCE

a. A right aim guides you to the right place.

b. Learn to hear Truth's constant invitation.

c. Life is different when your mind is different.

d. Discover the pure power of cosmic logic.

e. Courage comes to whoever really wants out.

f. Your real self and cosmic guidance are one.

g. As insight rises, so does beneficial action.

h. Think of mental silence as a perfect teacher.

i. As we lose earthly toys we gain cosmic gold.

j. All these facts build a reliable compass!

Chapter 5

ABOLISH HEARTACHE AND REGRET

249.   Q: I am in constant heartache over a broken love affair. How can I end the pain?

A: The pain in a broken romance can be ended instantly, provided you really want to end it. But there is a peculiar false pleasure in the pain. You unconsciously value this odd mixture of pleasure and pain; you love the thrill of its agitation. Ponder this as a first step.

250.   Q: Would you please explain a bit more?

A: Conscious sacrifice is necessary. Consciously sacrifice your heartache. Become aware of its pang and simply drop it. This interrupts its mechanical flow and finally ends it altogether. Experiment with this.

251.   Q: Then we must not seek an outside solution?

A: Just as the battle is within, so is the victory.

252.   Q: Please discuss unseen chains.

A: Said a teacher to his class, "To remove an inner chain you must first become aware of it. Otherwise you will live under the delusion that you have no chains, which is a terrible chain in itself." The teacher then asked, "Are you sometimes fearful that other people might become angry toward you?" As the students nodded the teacher said, "See? This is probably the first time you have had a clear look at this chain. Now we can proceed intelligently to remove it."

253. Q: I feel frustrated but don't know why.
A: You can live from contradictory rules imposed upon you by society or you can live freely from yourself, so how much effort will you make to see the difference in the two?

254. Q: How can we recognize a right course?
A: It comes first as a sensing, as when you feel the rightness of self-reliance. Then you read a book or hear a lecture which confirms the power and liberty of relying on yourself. Then by actually using your own resources you see that self-reliance is as right and as pleasurable as sunshine.

255. Q: How does lack of self-reliance lead us astray?
A: People are unable to distinguish between the attraction of human personality and an attraction toward truth itself. Truth is sky high above the hypnotic spell of cunning human personality. This error leads to the idolization of charming charlatans of various kinds who claim to understand life. Self-reliance erases the error.

256. Q: In spite of all our toys we are still miserable. Why?
A: Because you work so hard at it. Do you

74

realize how hard people work at being miserable? I will tell you one way in which they succeed. They call the evil the good and call the good the evil. Believe me, that is hard work, but anyone who persists will succeed overwhelmingly at being miserable.

257. Q: What is your counsel for meeting shocking news?

A: Shocking news can either liberate us or devastate us, depending upon a wish to understand or upon a wish to feel dramatic emotions.

258. Q: Please comment on gullibility.

A: One way to get hurt is to believe that human personalities and social organizations have the same kindly motives they claim to have.

259. Q: But this seems cynical. Should we not think the best of people?

A: Heaven help you if you think it best to call a wolf a lamb.

260. Q: Please explain a recent comment of yours in which you stated that we have chosen our own sad condition.

A: There was once a strange zoo in which all the animals were willing captives. Rather than live freely in the woods and mountains they preferred to take orders from the zoo keepers. This is the present state of humanity. And here is another incredible fact: An individual who has forsaken his right to think and act for himself will not believe in a thousand years that he has done just this.

261. Q: How do we unknowingly injure ourselves?

A: A person pays for deceptive behavior not only in the future because of the law of cause and effect, but also at the very moment the deception is practiced, for he pays by being the kind of nervous person he is.

262. Q: Since coming to these meetings I am more aware of my painful self-contradictions. I see the need for ending them. May we have a method?

A: Try to catch yourself playing a role in public. For instance, have you ever tried to appear confident and cheerful when you were inwardly scared and depressed? Try to observe yourself in this kind of contradiction. It creates an awakening jolt.

263. Q: Life is often so severe. What can I do when I can't take it any more?

A: You can use your condition profitably by seeing a healing fact. You can see that you are really being severe with yourself. When life is harsh with you it is exactly the same as harsh treatment of yourself, for your life and you are a single unit. Start to absorb this fact.

264. Q: Does this also mean that self-healing is the same as total life-healing? If I purify the source

of the stream I purify the entire stream?

A: Exactly. See how swiftly you learn? See how you can answer your own question? What a nice way to live. What a confident way!

265. Q: Where do we go wrong in seeking happiness?

A: A miserable man heard of a paradise kingdom where everyone lived happily and abundantly. Traveling to its border he requested admittance. The gate keeper told him, "Like most people, you misunderstand. Everyone here discovered his own inner paradise before coming here. Sir, let me ask you a question. Do you really believe that a mere change in exterior surroundings can make you happy?"

266. Q: My particular problem is impulsive feelings. They recklessly distort my reason.

A: Substituting emotion for logic is like burning a book instead of reading it. Calm logic enables us to read and understand and command any circumstance. Do not permit fiery feelings to burn up your opportunities to command life.

267. Q: But I feel powerless before impulsiveness.

A: That simply means you can continue to study until changing things. See how gently and kindly these teachings treat you? They do not condemn you for anything; they simply encourage you to succeed in one success at a time.

268. Q: We are urged to free ourselves from the past. Could you please simplify the method?

A: Suppose a friend is taking a motion picture film of you when your foot slips and you tumble down a hillside. You rise somewhat shaken but unhurt. When viewing the film later on you feel pokes of pain over the experience. Your friend reminds, "This is only a film. It can't cause pain unless you wrongly connect yourself with it." See the great secret of liberation? Break mental movies of the past and pain disappears.

269. Q: You once remarked that spiritual matters are scientifically certain. What did you mean?

A: Just as the rising sun must end darkness, so must dawning inner light put an end to unhappiness.

270. Q: What practical benefit arrives by living in this new kind of consciousness?

A: When living unconsciously you never know you are heading for disaster until the trap springs shut on you, until you must now pay the price in shock and worry. Conscious living is different, for when knowing a trap when seeing one it is easily avoided.

271. Q: Please continue.

A: It is a fascinating adventure to escape the trap. And it can be done, providing we ask the right question with enough force. Beneath their daily activities most people dimly ask the right

78

question, "How can I get out—I mean really get out?" I will show you how to really get out. You get out by using the fact that you are not out. What does this mean? It means that your very awareness of being trapped is the power that breaks the trap.

272.   Q: That is not clear to me.
     A: You see, when a person's pain reaches a certain intensity—*and he has even a small but sincere wish to understand his suffering*—something cracks. This is the breaking of the trap. This is the cracking of the hard shell of self-concern which the sufferer has fearfully refused to surrender up to now. The intense agony creates such a crisis that he must choose either ego-abandonment or choose to remain in his unbearable condition.

273.   Q: What happens if he chooses ego-surrender?
     A: As I said, something breaks, something opens. The man now sees something totally different; he is a bit more conscious. The next crisis must then be met with the wish to understand even more, which causes more cracking, followed by more self-release. By repeating this conscious process over the months an individual gets out of the trap and stays out.

274.   Q: I am frustrated by myself.
     A: Frustration over ourselves falls away as we cease to believe in illusions about ourselves.

275.   Q: I have done so many terrible things in the past I feel I may be beyond rescue.

A: Who did these terrible things? Unconscious and reckless forces which took you over. They behaved badly so often in your name that you identified with them, that is, you labeled yourself as terrible. That mere label is now your wrong identity. Drop the label and everything becomes free and clear at last. Never mind if you fail to understand all this just now. We will work together on it.

276.   Q: How can spontaneity replace struggle?

A: A teacher observed that one of his students was still struggling to make self-will do the work of cosmic power. The teacher told the pupil, "The inner spirit soars all by itself when we cease to believe in our own decorated but useless wings."

277.   Q: I have been pondering a remark you made last week. You said we must get rid of false goodness based on a false sense of duty. Examples, please.

A: False goodness is a terrible burden. It crushes those who practice religion mechanically. Also, some people think they are being good when they are merely being gullible. This occurs when they yield to sweet words from tricky people. The harvest is regret and resentment. Real goodness has no such weaknesses.

278. Q: How does delusion cause destruction?

A: Two clashing men always believe it is the clash between two real worlds, when it is merely the clash of two weird worlds of egotism, both craving to loot life.

279. Q: Shame and regret over past behavior is a constant underground torment. Can it be banished?

A: It is banished by banishing a false sense of time. The real you is free right now. Like a demon running away from an angel, shame vanishes from the life of whoever lives in the reality of the present moment.

280. Q: How can I conquer a feeling of despair?

A: Despair is conquered by daring to drop the mechanical emotion of which it is composed. First, be clearly aware of the feeling. Next, dare to drop its false pleasure. Yes, there is false pleasure in despair, for you would rather feel despair than face the emptiness of no feeling at all. But let the emptiness be there, and watch what happens. Try to drop despair the moment it appears and you will see how it does not want to give you up. So you must give it up. Do so.

281. Q: I have taken the first step of seeing my actual state of psychic imprisonment. What next?

A: An innocent man was imprisoned by political enemies. Escape seemed impossible until he made a curious discovery. By shaking the door in a certain manner the hinges became loose. After several days of secret shaking the hinges fell away, permitting escape. With cosmic knowledge we can shake ourselves loose of everything imprisoning, including hidden heartaches.

282. Q: Inform us of a harmful emotion to guard against.

A: Feeling power over others. This emotion flares up in a person of authority when others must come to him for something, or when he can deny them something. It is doubly dangerous because its egotistical thrill is taken as a positive feeling. It is in fact a negative force, not far from arrogance and revenge.

283. Q: My world always seems about to collapse.

A: The real world can never collapse, so the only question is, do you want the real or the fantasy world?

284. Q: How can we tell whether we are living in the fantasy world?

A: If you suffer and secretly like it.

285. Q: Anxiety is written on the faces of everyone, even those who are supposed to have the answers. Does personal liberation provide permanent poise?

A: Inner liberty can be compared with a former actor no longer forced to play awkward and unpleasant roles, no longer fearful that others will see through his shallow performance.

286. Q: Suffering seems so powerful, so permanent.

A: Listen carefully to what I am going to tell you, then act upon it. Suffering cannot endure unless the sufferer unconsciously glorifies it for self-serving reasons, so a lack of cooperation with suffering will end it.

287. Q: You mean we actually encourage our own pain?

A: Yes, for it seems to confirm cherished but illusory identities, such as being a persecuted martyr or of being a neglected soul who will be rewarded by God in some vague and future heaven. This is terrible egotism. The ego does not want to surrender these false identities, but you must do so.

288. Q: What is the correct way to speak about heaven?

A: The kingdom of heaven is within, and consists of the absence of time and egotism. It can be personally experienced.

289. Q: Help our understanding of all this!

A: Your willingness to understand will open the gate. What stands in the way of willingness? Pride? Fear of new facts? Hostility? A reluctance to let go? Dare to remove them. The gate will open all by itself.

290. Q: Why do we bump into everything?

A: When closing our eyes to what we don't want to see we also close them to what we need to see. There is no simpler explanation of why we bump into everything.

291. Q: Last week you spoke of natural protection from conniving people. How is this protection won?

A: When you know human nature you know the real reason anyone does anything, which protects you from everyone.

292. Q: I have had a severe anguish over the last few months. Can I hope for relief in time?

A: Never wait for time to heal sorrow. It cannot and will not do so. Sorrow supposedly healed by time is still there, like a ghost who glides regularly out of his hiding place to haunt the victim. You can and should drop sorrow right now, and right now means right now. Time cannot prevent you from doing this once you understand the power of cosmic consciousness over time. This is not really a mysterious process. It is something you can learn to do, regardless of how tightly you seem gripped by sorrow. Start by reviewing and pondering these ideas.

293. Q: This conquers gloom?

A: Gloom has no power over a man except that which the man himself gives it through lack of psychic knowledge.

294. Q: Please clear my mind. I want to find this higher life, but relatives and friends act as if I am betraying them, which makes me feel guilty.

A: If you rightly decide to break out of your habitual life, and other people feel hurt or threatened by your necessary decision, you are not responsible for their wrong feelings.

295. Q: It is clear that obedience to truth is our first requirement. How will success in this affect our human relations?

A: You will see that you are not required to obey anyone whose behavior demands that you take care of him.

296. Q: How should we act toward unpleasant people?

A: Unpleasantness from others can be used wisely for psychic maturity. The sarcastic or cruel person shocks you. Why? Simply because you fail to see many things. Try to see a cruel person as scared, which he is. Try to see your real nature as above cruel attacks, which it is.

297. Q: Why are we exploited by others and how can it be stopped?

A: To the degree that we seek consolation in daydreams we will be exploited by other people who do the same.

298. Q: Last night I suddenly realized that gullibility is simply the absence of the self-knowledge we must obtain.

A: A young and innocent deer was told by some wolves that green grass and fresh water were available inside their cave. It did not sound logical to the deer, but being hungry, he entered the cave. Fortunately, he discovered his error before the wolves had time to block his exit. No one is ever led astray by anything but his own lack of cosmic logic. Those who face this fact will never again be led astray by anyone.

299. Q: Some people find it hard to believe these teachings when they say that man is mechanical instead of conscious.

A: Most human beings spend their lives making mechanical reactions to exterior challenges. Just press any psychic button and you can make a man respond with irritation or shock or tears or envy. Not developed beyond the mechanical stage he is the slave of everyone who presses the buttons. Nothing is easier to prove than a man's mechanical nature. Just tell him he is mechanical instead of conscious. Watch his reaction.

300. Q: Please comment on agitation.

A: Agitation is an impostor. It is a false emotion which deceives a person into feeling alive and active. Cease to love agitation. Just cease to love it. Your real nature can then communicate its calm.

301. Q: We must cease to be victims of ourselves.

A: One of the strangest facts about man is

the way he takes truth as his enemy and takes error as his friend. He is like a dazed soldier on a battle-field who mistakes enemy soldiers as his comrades. The cunning enemy then keeps his illusion alive in order to use him for their own evil purposes. Only by awakening from his error can he escape.

302. Q: How can we end self-damaging behavior?

A: Look at self-defeating behavior, and when you *really recognize* it as self-defeating it will not repeat itself.

303. Q: As a doctor I sometimes slide into conversations with patients about spiritual topics. I observe a strange and sad condition. The more troubled the patient the more he tries to convince me of his happiness.

A: Strange and sad is a good description. Pretending to know the truth when we can really have it is like a hungry man standing in an apple orchard and pretending to eat.

304. Q: I am in a severe condition causing emotional turmoil. I don't know how to end the condition. I don't know what to do.

A: Know that it is possible to end the heartache in a condition without ending the condition itself.

305. Q: How can this be accomplished?

A: The way to turn internal horrors into internal heavens is to make the horrors conscious.

This means we must never turn away from the friendly facts which help us do this.

306. Q: That is our problem—we prefer fantasies to facts.

A: Disliking facts because they fail to agree with our fantasies is as sensible as getting nervous because two and two make four.

307. Q: May we have a friendly fact to absorb right now?

A: A first step toward self-rescue is to stop demanding that rescue should look like your preconceived ideas of it.

308. Q: Help us to react rightly to life.

A: You can learn to walk past your own wrong reactions. Suppose someone behaves badly toward you. Your usual response is to feel hurt or feel anger. This time you will do something different. Immediately walk past those habitual reactions. Refuse to get involved with them, just as you might walk past a rioting mob without taking part in its madness. Increase your ability for doing this by seeing that wrong reactions are wrong for *you* by seeing them as self-punishments instead of as self-rewards.

309. Q: How can we really learn from experience?

A: To learn from an unhappy experience means to realize how a personal negative trait caused a personal negative event.

310. Q: Why is it so important to study cosmic laws?

A: Because you are composed of them. A study of cosmic laws is a study of yourself. A story will illustrate. A farmer was irritated over an inferior fruit tree in his orchard. He blamed the former owner of the farm. Then he suddenly remembered that he had planted the tree himself, many years ago. See how vital it is to see how we cause our own results?

311. Q: I believe you are saying that we can stop causing trouble to ourselves. What a great destination.

A: So dare to keep traveling, never settling down, for the next needed oasis is out there, awaiting your arrival.

REMEMBER THESE VITAL THOUGHTS

a. Self-reliance is a natural power and pleasure.

b. Let a crisis fall upon your wish to understand it.

c. Claim your right to think and act for yourself.

d. Nothing is more practical than esotericism.

e. Your real nature is free from past mistakes.

f. Your true world is never in danger of collapse.

g. When suffering is not glorified it vanishes.

h. Painful gullibility is banished by cosmic insight.

i. These friendly facts can make anyone whole.

j. The oasis is out there, waiting for you!

Chapter 6

MENTAL MAGIC FOR REAL RICHES

312. Q: I find it hard to acquire higher ideas.

A: Suppose you wish to place a table in space occupied by a chair. You must first remove the chair. Suppose you wish to stand in a place occupied by another person. The other person must first depart. Here is the lesson. A negative attitude must first depart in order to make space for a true viewpoint.

313. Q: How can I develop my capacity to perceive more?

A: Dare to no longer tolerate those thoughts which have no intention of receiving perception.

314. Q: You urge us to do the possible. What is it?

A: Since it is possible to live in this world without trading away our mental integrity, why not do so?

315. Q: I need more information about the difference between an ordinary mind and a conscious mind.

A: I will give you something to think about. An ordinary mind thinks back and forth, indecisively, while a conscious mind understands and acts instantly. Its understanding and action are the same thing. When understanding hot weather you act effortlessly toward a drink of cool water.

When having even a small insight into your talent for self-freedom your very insight is action toward inner liberty.

316. Q: May we have a method for using mental energy wisely?

A: Think of how we constantly insist that other people should treat us better. Now think how all this power of insistence could be channeled into making us inwardly right.

317. Q: How can we attain real intelligence?

A: Real intelligence exists in the absence of the need to appear intelligent. I wonder whether any of you in this class see the depth of this simple idea.

318. Q: We will try to see it. This leads me to the question of how we can end wrong thinking.

A: The sure way to end wrong thinking is to think carefully about your thinking. Try to see what it is really like, how it causes you to behave in certain ways, try to see how mental movement causes exterior results. Use the mind to empower the mind.

319. Q: Please explain a law of mental science. Why does an unhappy mind meet so many unhappy experiences?

A: A thought reproduces its own nature in visible form, just as the shape of the object decides the shape of the shadow.

320. Q: Changing the viewpoint is necessary but hard.

A: Start with this helpful information. A hardened viewpoint is incapable of seeing anything outside of itself. It is like a searchlight at night that points in one direction only. We change our views a thousand times a year, but not noticing this we fail to see the possibility of changing a present view. We drop a useless viewpoint when actually seeing its uselessness.

321. Q: Finding right answers and making right decisions. That is where I fail.

A: What happens when a confused mind tries to find an answer? It finds a confused answer. What happens when a confused mind makes a decision? It makes a confused decision. Don't you think it essential to clear your mind?

322. Q: Yes, but what must I do?

A: You must want a clear mind more than you want the false pleasures derived from thinking as you now do.

323. Q: What do you mean by false pleasures?

A: There are many kinds but I will define one of them. A false pleasure is anything that appears to make you right in the eyes of others but actually keeps you secretly nervous over your wrongness.

324. Q: What do you mean by spiritual talent?

A: Your true mind has talent for avoiding human opinion to get straight to the point. Wise men and women eagerly welcome the point, especially when it is contrary to their opinion.

325. Q: Please explain how intellectualism limits us.

A: A child on a swing realizes he is not moving away from his fixed position. He knows that his attachment is a limiting factor in which forward is always followed by backward. But a man living in fixed intellectualism fails to see the same law at work. He deludes himself into believing that social schemes or religious activities can swing him toward satisfaction. But only detachment from mental fixation can do that.

326. Q: Then intellectualism is powerless to uplift life?

A: Intellectualism can solve human problems about as much as a typewriter can write letters all by itself.

327. Q: How are we led astray by our own illogic?

A: Nothing is more illogical than for a man to believe he can change his life without changing himself, for he is his life.

328. Q: Why do people react with dread and dislike to new and unfamiliar teachings which could rescue them?

A: The teachings challenge people to venture beyond their limited worlds to something far richer, but weak minds prefer to remain lazy and smug.

329. Q: Give us something to clear the mental mist.

A: A man takes his own viewpoint as the only world in existence, which is like taking earth as the only planet in the universe. Look beyond yourself! Feel the meaning in these three words and you will generate power enough to carry you to the cosmic world.

330. Q: How does the mind go wrong unknowingly?

A: A man can believe he sees something when in fact there is nothing real to see. Perhaps he hears a speech about politics or economics. If it agrees with his acquired viewpoints he declares it is real and sensible. If it opposes his borrowed beliefs he rejects it as nonsense. In either case he is simply seeing his own touchy notions which he wrongly feels makes him individualistic. He must learn that the Real resides above self-pleasing ideas.

331. Q: How would you describe a false value?

A: Anything contributing to a wrong way of life, anything maintaining inner conflict. This includes a hope for external peace without internal transformation, unnatural pleasure in having power over other people, depending upon habitual thought instead of cosmic principles.

332. Q: What is a result of winning cosmic consciousness?

A: Things which now seem so important and so overwhelming will be seen as nonessential. They will be as out of your mind as last year's storm. This includes worry over your business career and concern over your security within the family.

333. Q: We have given considerable thought to the topic of unconscious slavery which you covered last week. Do you mean that a psychic slave never knows he is one?

A: His unconsciousness *is* his slavery. This is why it is difficult to teach unhappy people. Never having sighted their psychic chains they deny their existence. Those who deny must continue to cry.

334. Q: So admitting our chains is necessary for cutting them off. What will be a typical result of doing this?

A: You will no longer feel threatened by the rude or unpleasant facial expressions of other people.

335. Q: What can help our esoteric education?

A: It helps to understand a certain peculiarity of the mind. The moment a man acquires a new piece of knowledge he assumes he now knows everything possible to know. That is like thinking a tree has only one leaf. So vanity blocks further development. Guard against this.

336. Q: Our minds are so mischievous!

A: The sure way to stop the mind from playing unpleasant tricks on you is to command it with the power of these principles.

337. Q: By wrong thoughts do you mean self-harming ideas?

A: It can never be any other way. Wrong thoughts persuade you that you want many injurious things, such as striking back after a supposed insult. They also persuade you that you don't want many things, such as a truly independent mind. They accomplish this with the lie that human authority is superior to cosmic insight.

338. Q: Why do higher teachings place so much emphasis on mental clarity instead of on finding God, Truth, Reality?

A: Because a confused mind can find only confused beliefs about God, Truth, Reality. It is tragic error to think that a disorderly mind can discover that which is above riotous thought.

339. Q: How can we correct the error and attain a clear mind?

A: Have the courage to see and dissolve contradiction in oneself. Can a truly spiritual mind pretend to others to have the answers to human problems while not having the answers to its own entanglements? No. Can a truly decent mind outwardly disagree with violence while taking private pleasure in it? No.

340. Q: My observation of myself and others has shown me something. I clearly see how our own minds prevent the facts from reaching and refreshing us.

A: Yes. What happens to pure water when poured into a muddy cup?

341. Q: How can we attain real maturity?

A: Never identify yourself as being mentally or spiritually mature, for the fewer ideas you have about yourself the more mature you will be. Do you know people who subtly or openly hint how mature they are? How mature are they? Real maturity resides above the level of self-flattering self-labels.

342. Q: We assume we are choosing helpful thoughts, but they turn out harmful. How is this corrected?

A: Suppose you stand at a distance and study twelve apples, six real and six artificial. You can tell the difference only by coming closer. How strong is your interest in coming closer to your own mind?

343. Q: What do you mean by a higher viewpoint?

A: What twisted self-interest calls failure is called a huge success by a sensible mind. Perhaps you hope to meet someone, maybe an attractive man or woman, but nothing comes of it. You call it failure. Later you realize that a relationship with him or her could have produced nothing but grief. Now you see your very failure as a success.

344. Q: How can I use my mind to build a clear mind?

A: Since the mind is an advice-giving machine, ask yourself, "What kind of advice am I giving myself?"

345. Q: It puzzled me for awhile but I finally understand a point you made. You said a first requirement for self-newness was to become disenchanted with the rewards of this world.

A: Disenchanted, weary, dismayed—use any term you like. A man remains entangled with the world until reaching a certain point in his esoteric education. He finally sees that another world exists, *a world not made by his personal and habitual thoughts.*

346. Q: We assume we understand our minds, but social chaos proves that it is only an assumption.

A: The only reason the activities of the world are chaotic is because the activities of the mind are neglected.

347. Q: What is the relationship between awareness and intelligence—I mean authentic intelligence?

A: Awareness and intelligence are the same thing. For instance, only intelligence can see and acknowledge a negative character trait, such as resistance to facts. Stupidity can never admit it is wrong, which is why it remains wrong.

348. Q: Then pure awareness of a negative trait cures it?

A: Magically. When seeing a negative trait without self-defense or self-condemnation you see it with a clearness far above ordinary thinking, self-centered thinking. This is cosmic sight which is free from all negative traits.

349. Q: My aim is to eventually grasp all this.

A: Your aim is more noble than the stars.

350. Q: How is cosmic vision superior to the usual viewpoint?

A: Cosmic vision sees everything quite differently than ordinary vision. For example, an ordinary man looks out and sees a public figure as a hero or a leader. But someone with cosmic vision looks out at the same public figure and sees a hypocrite or a psychopath. Only cosmic vision sees things as they are.

351. Q: Please say something about preparation, I mean, inner preparation for eventual insight.

A: You prepare by collecting facts. This enables you to catch your first glimpse inside the cosmic castle when the door swings open briefly from time to time.

352. Q: You once advised us to proceed logically. How?

A: Proceed logically from one fact to the next. Make right connections. Suppose you start with the fact that even your own confusions cannot block self-liberty. That encouraging fact can reveal the informative fact that higher help is available. Connect this with the third fact that you must learn to distinguish between real and false help. This is a powerful procedure.

353.   Q: I am bothered by so many things!
        A: No, you are bothered by just one thing. The next time something bothers you, see that it is really your own misunderstanding mind.

354.   Q: We need new thinking. How can we jolt and break up our hardened thinking habits?
        A: You live your life from ideas which you take as right for you—from what you *take* as right for you. But how strange that these ideas that you take as right have produced nothing but nervousness and helplessness. Ponder that peculiar situation. Let it jolt you.

355.   Q: We need a new start.
        A: You can start anew any moment, such as right now.

356.   Q: How?
        A: Drop habitual thought.

357.   Q: But how do we drop habitual thought?
        A: By dropping it.

358.   Q: I need to make right decisions.

A: Decide every morning that you will try to live in this new and invisible world, this world which has nothing to do with society's ravings. Do this even if you have no idea of what it means. You will eventually see that this new world is your own new mind.

359. Q: I made a note of a lesson given last night. It urged us to work in the right psychic place. May we have an example of working in the right place?

A: Truth is never obscure. The mind is obscure. So where is the right place to work to win clarity? Study your mind.

360. Q: Society builds haunted houses, calling them castles. Is there intelligent action anywhere?

A: Only individual action toward spiritual health is intelligent. For example, you have to live with your own mind. Can you think of anything more intelligent than making it a good mind to live with?

361. Q: Is it a fact that we consent to our own foolish actions?

A: Is it a fact that a foolish thought creates a foolish action?

362. Q: Yes, that is obvious. My own wrong thought was the consent.

A: Be grateful that there is one thing Truth will not do. It will not approve or participate in our harmful actions.

363. Q: How can we end mental wandering?

A: We think about foolish things when lacking the knowledge or the courage to think about intelligent things. If a man is lost in the jungle it makes no sense for him to think about the colors of the entangling vines. He must think about the way out.

364. Q: How can we banish injurious ideas?

A: Add beneficial ideas to your mind and they will finally banish harmful ideas, just as color banishes drabness.

365. Q: How can we melt hardened, harmful thoughts?

A: It is agonizing to be clutched by hardened thoughts, whether self-flattering ideas or religious doctrines or obsessive ambitions. Two people quarrel. Both are hardened by prideful belief that the other should apologize first, so both suffer from their own hardness. Such thoughts are melted by studying the whole process of thought, which we are now doing.

366. Q: Apparently we are unaware of our cosmic opportunities.

A: These ideas are perfect opportunities for people who realize there is something wrong with their lives but don't as yet know what to do about it.

367. Q: What specific opportunity are we neglecting.

A: The opportunity to examine and comprehend your own mind. Trying to command life without studying one's own mind is like trying to play a piano without studying music.

368. Q: You say we must let agony rise from the unconscious to the conscious level. But that seems to add even more agony.

A: To see a pain consciously is no worse than living with it unconsciously. Like a physical wound, it is just as painful in the dark as in the light, but we don't see it. So evasion or suppression only perpetuates agony. Remember this one point. Remember that conscious pain is no worse than unseen pain, though it does operate in a different way, which brings release.

369. Q: How can we hear the ideas we need?

A: Imagine a schoolboy in class who has little interest in the topic under study, so his mind wanders. Later that day a topic of great interest to him is introduced by the teacher. The boy comes alive! When a person has an interest in higher lessons, they will be heard, sooner or later.

370. Q: Please provide an example of immature thinking.

A: Using the wrongdoing of other people as an excuse for our own bad behavior. Only a weak and childish mind does that. And it can do it while insisting it does not do it.

371. Q: I am still puzzled regarding the path to peace.

A: A simple procedure clearly understood and acted on has great power for self-transformation. One such simple procedure is to turn your mind in a new direction. These principles make such a turning possible. You can turn from worry to self-command, from loneliness to self-completion.

372. Q: We waste our lives in trivialities.

A: Then stop. No day is wasted in which you make at least one attempt to be aware of and to break your usual ways of thinking.

373. Q: Then the secret is to invite right thoughts?

A: Just as you would invite pleasant guests into your home. It is a right and pleasant thought that new energies within can be awakened and used, a good thought that the heavy hypnosis of dread and gloom can be blown away by the winds of consciousness.

374. Q: What is a specific benefit of inner exploration?

A: A knight in armor was told about some fierce dragons living in a gigantic cave. Bravely exploring the cave the knight saw that the dragons existed only in fearful imaginations. This means we need not fear wild and menacing thoughts, regardless of how real they seem. They vanish in the light of consciousness.

375. Q: And we can actually win this new mental clarity?

A: The ignorance which causes painful blundering can end just as surely as rain ends the land's dryness.

376. Q: To think for myself! That is it!

A: It is weakness to believe that others can think for us, vanity to believe we can think for others, and relieving wisdom to know we can think for ourselves.

377. Q: What advice does a beginner need?

A: A story was told about a spiritual seeker who roamed from one land to another, seeking the key to inner insight. He finally found a wise man who told him, "Learn to think in another way."

OUTSTANDING LESSONS IN REVIEW

a. Make mental room for healing principles.

b. Thoughts reproduce themselves in physical form.

c. It is a noble aim to wish for a clear mind.

d. Today, resolve to see something beyond yourself!

e. Cosmic consciousness clears away all worries.

f. An esoteric education creates a commanding mind.

g. Only cosmic vision sees things as they are.

h. Try to catch a glimpse of the cosmic castle.

i. Let right ideas chase out harmful ideas.

j. Learn to think in the celestial way.

Chapter 7

GAIN TRUE POWER AND ENERGY

378. Q: Recently you used the phrase *cosmic confidence.* May we hear more?

A: Your real nature is confidence itself. Cosmic confidence is complete, having all resources in itself. It is like a competent captain of a ship who never needs to ask directions from anyone else aboard.

379. Q: The idea of self-command appeals to me, but I have little actual command.

A: Having the idea of self-command is a good and necessary first step. But a man can think about the idea of self-command and still be a slave to his own unhappiness. Self-command resides above the level of mere ideas. A book can contain hundreds of right ideas, but the book has no power to live them out. Self-command is attained by rising above the mental level to the level of cosmic consciousness.

380. Q: What specific strength does a free mind possess?

A: A free mind cannot be intimidated by anyone or anything. People never see how often and how easily they are intimidated during a single day. It might be caused by a frown from someone, bad news, a sharp word from someone in authority. Freedom from intimidation is one part of inner heaven.

381. Q: I belong to a small study group of about twenty people. May I have an idea to take back to them?

A: Self-rescue requires considerable energy, and we can save valuable energy by not going along with negative feelings.

382. Q: How can we apply these ideas in a crisis?

A: Connect a crisis with something you have learned. People forget to do this, losing the psychic silver they could have had. An emotional crisis offers a special opportunity, as when you lose someone important to your sense of security.

383. Q: In other words we must apply knowledge to the crisis.

A: Knowledge is light, and light is what you really need, not sentimental comfort and distraction.

384. Q: But strong emotion prevents us from remembering what we must do.

A: Which is exactly why an effort against such an obstacle returns such a rich reward. It is no test of psychic strength to work on yourself in clear weather. Remember and apply these ideas right in the middle of the emotional storm. The more it knocks you around the more strength you can win from it.

385. Q: We are so filled with doubts!

A: Have no doubts but that the cosmic

medicine will do its healing work, providing you really take it.

386. Q: Most of us run away from our problems.
      A: Which is why they are neither understood nor ended. It is extremely useful to endure an uncomfortable state with a watchful mind, simply trying to see what it is all about. If you want self-transforming, self-knowledge, this is the way to acquire it.

387. Q: Please repeat that idea in different words.
      A: Self-transformation comes by enduring an inner storm consciously. This means you must stand aside as an impartial observer instead of just being the storm. Then, many interesting experiences will come your way.

388. Q: Could you be specific about this?
      A: The world which now seems real and comfortable to you will become strange and uncomfortable. The cosmic world which now appears unreal and uncomfortable to you will become solid and reliable.

389. Q: How can we improve our spiritual diet?
      A: Anyone can obtain healthier spiritual food, such as sensible thoughts, by first noticing the deficiencies in his present daily diet. Does the present diet really make you less anxious and more confident? Ask yourself questions like that. Anyone becoming conscious of inferior spiritual

foods is aroused to find something better.

390. Q: We are not always aware of areas needing correction. Please discuss one such area.

A: To imagine that we understand something is not the same as understanding it. When imagination is used wrongly it becomes a powerful force for self-deception. Have you ever seen someone angrily deny his anger? That is a good example of how ego-protecting imagination prevents us from seeing our actual condition.

391. Q: Then when imagination is used incorrectly it becomes a wall which keeps us out of our cosmic castle?

A: That is correct. The wall consists of many bricks, including imaginary virtues, imaginary strengths, imaginary goals. Do you know one of the hardest bricks in the wall? It is when a man imagines he is not imagining!

392. Q: I am increasingly aware of my weakness and dependency. What is a curative idea?

A: When glimpsing a new truth you need not seek the approval of anyone else before accepting it as your own.

393. Q: Please comment on real conscience.

A: Weakness has no real conscience. Real strength has no cruelty.

394. Q: You have observed me over the months.

What personal advice do you have for me?

A: Avoid wasting energy on trivial matters. Avoid triviality in favor of the important, just as a space explorer passes small and dry worlds to finally land on a large and beautiful planet.

395. Q: Please describe cosmic power.

A: Cosmic power within the individual is natural and relaxed, fully adequate in all circumstances, for it contains no defensive or offensive elements so common in neurotic states.

396. Q: How can we act from ourselves, I mean, from our real and sensible nature?

A: Most human beings act from mere memory, while believing they are acting from themselves. They really act from parents and friends and everyone else they have met in the past. To act from oneself it is necessary to see the simple fact that one is not his acquired memories. Imagine an actor who grows weary of playing a well-rehearsed role, so he gives up the theater to live his own natural life. It is like that.

397. Q: What can we do for ourselves today?

A: Do something dynamic by becoming aware of the simple power of clear thinking. This awareness arises after you are fully convinced of the weakness of muddled thinking.

398. Q: You are saying that no one tries to escape the swamp until first admitting he is in one.

A: Stated in another way, a man living in a swamp will feel miserable no matter how often he tells himself he dwells in a pleasant meadow.

399. Q: I need someone to be brave for me.

A: No, no. You must be brave for yourself. You can be. Do you know what it means to be brave? It means to voluntarily endure the shock of losing wrong ideas you have about yourself and about life. Think energetically about this definition of bravery, then act on it.

400. Q: I need more strength for climbing the mountain.

A: One characteristic of a sheeplike mind is its refusal to step forward all alone. Such a weak mind always wants another person to lead or accompany it. So one condition for climbing the mountain is to not expect other people to go with you. See the necessity for climbing, for that will give you strength to climb alone.

401. Q: Please describe the path to self-conquest.

A: Self-conquest is the voluntary detection and abandonment of everything within which we feel is unnatural.

402. Q: When will our weakness be replaced by strength?

A: When you see something you do not as yet see. I will give your psychic eyesight an exercise. Your inner essence has total power over worldly chaos. It has total power over the world because it is not part of the world, just as a shining star remains unaffected by earthly storms. See this.

403.   Q: I appreciate an explanation you made last week. Part of me was reluctant to hear it, but another part sensed its rightness. You said we must choose true knowledge over false comfort.

A: A scared man surrounded by a thousand comforting voices is still a scared man. By refusing false comfort he could learn what it means to not be scared.

404.   Q: Please explain a recent comment. You said that the real can grow only at the expense of the artificial.

A: Self-realness comes only by dropping self-fakery. Both cannot occupy psychic space at the same time.

405.   Q: Why do we fail to see our own fakery?

A: Because it is so enormous. You think that self-fakery is a small rock on the mountain, when in fact it is the entire mountain. Not everyone can bear the shock of seeing this, but those who do will remove their mountainous burdens.

406.   Q: Realization is power. Please tell us about something we can realize.

A: Realize that it is possible to be with agitated people who have lost self-command while remaining in perfect command of yourself.

407. Q: How can we escape feelings of weakness?

A: Weakness handled with an alert mind turns to strength. Suppose you suffer a loss of some kind, making you feel weak and sad. Wake up! Refuse the feeling. Make it absolutely clear that you will have nothing to do with the weakness. A new feeling of strength will come.

408. Q: Courage and confidence. There is where we fail.

A: Real courage is the act of entering into one's own despair, no longer avoiding it, in order to understand and end it. Then you realize the existence of cosmic confidence which resides far above the level of ordinary thought.

409. Q: I am dismayed at the number of things I cannot understand.

A: It is possible to be bewildered over the meaning of something without being discouraged. This is an advanced state of strength. It means that you are controlling your weak parts instead of them controlling you.

410. Q: I want my life back!

A: Every action taken to regain your own life, such as not compromising with deceitful people, produces more wisdom and energy for regaining even more of your own life.

411. Q: I often feel drained of energy by relatives and friends. What about this feeling?

A: The purpose of society is to lean on you while pretending to give you something. Your purpose should be to refuse it by standing apart.

412. Q: Why do we reject the healing medicine?

A: Because of the mental habit of calling medicine vinegar. The caller is quite wrong, but his distaste for vinegar is stronger than his logic. So he shuns the necessary experience of tasting for himself. But here is a curious point. Medicine does in fact taste like vinegar at first because he is not used to it. But after awhile its taste is supremely marvelous.

413. Q: It is strengthening just to realize that truth is supreme.

A: Falsehood cannot dim the truth any more than a drop of water can extinguish the sun.

414. Q: How can we make weakness desire strength?

A: Weakness can never desire strength. A sheep can never desire to be an eagle, for it has no idea of what it means to be an eagle. The weak masses of humanity do not want real strength, for being unable to recognize it they cannot value it. But the tiny point of real strength within a person can be developed.

415. Q: What neglected power can we develop?

A: Give attention to the power of attention. Attend eagerly to cosmically constructive ideas.

I will give you one right now. Truth solves all problems, but remember that it does *in a way you cannot presently see.* Deep attention to that can reveal a new world.

416. Q: We want to climb the mountain but have our attention on the desert!

A: People simply fail to attend to their own psychic ascension. This causes a wide variety of delusions. As an example, those who are most certain they can save the world are those who are least capable of saving themselves.

417. Q: Dozens of daily decisions keep us exhausted!

A: When no longer involved with false beliefs we are wonderfully free of making difficult decisions. You are then like a citizen of an oppressive country who rejects its treacherous codes to escape to a free land. He is no longer involved in the tense decisions of his former country.

418. Q: How can we be more efficient in the use of time when on the inner quest?

A: It is interesting and profitable to ask at the end of the day, "How many minutes belonged to me and how many belonged to negative forces which took me over?"

419. Q: I am too weak to conquer my own negative forces.

A: Imagine a mob of bullies who terrorize a

weak and fearful man who walks by. The bullies are able to bluff and dominate the weak man only because they see his weakness. But if he becomes strong, they will also see that, and will leave him alone. Negative forces are bullies which have power only because of individual weakness. They flee when seeing cosmic power.

420. Q: But I have no cosmic command.
A: It would be correct to say that you don't have present contact with your own cosmic command. You are in this class to make contact.

421. Q: Help us break a psychic chain.
A: Self-flattering labels maintain self-slavery, as with someone with neurotic compulsions who calls them noble ambitions or religious convictions.

422. Q: What does it mean to be in command of one's own life?
A: When cosmic power is in charge of your life, you are in charge of your own life.

423. Q: How is this cosmic command attained?
A: By honestly seeing that your life is presently controlled by foreign forces. These alien forces can include self-centered thinking, a public appearance of having self-command which is merely a stage-performance, reckless emotions, crying over life instead of studying it with an aim to change things.

424. Q: How does this attract cosmic command?

A: It starts the change. A man who really sees he is living in a cave soon starts to search for the way out.

425. Q: You say that cosmic power must take over and command our lives. But we object to something taking us over.

A: You are taken over by yourself, by your real nature. The objection comes from the foreign forces which fear you are escaping their dark domination. Ignore their powerless threats and continue to escape.

426. Q: How can we release our creative capacity in both everyday and spiritual matters?

A: Start by seeing what blocks it. A chief barrier is trying to get personal credit and applause from your actions. God, Truth, Reality does not give such shallow rewards. The essence of religion teaches this but no one wants to see it. Your true creative capacity is impersonal, cosmic, and realization of this releases it.

427. Q: How are healing powers attracted?

A: Healing powers are ready to respond to the man or woman who takes the initiative in inner work.

428. Q: We sometimes wonder whether we can make it.

A: You can make it. The ray of light can

117

break through years of hard resistance, through thousands of mistakes. This is not simply an encouragement. It is fact.

429. Q: Suppose a self-deceived person applies these ideas with as much sincerity as possible. What happens next?

A: Sooner or later it will occur to him that Reality is neither deceived by his pretenses nor intimidated by his arrogance. At this point he feels both a sense of defeat and a sense of new strength. It is the false self which senses the defeat, and the dawning new nature which senses the strength. This double sensing will be accompanied by profound emotions, enabling him to remember and value the experience. Self-transformation has begun.

430. Q: What responsibility do I have and not have?

A: Do what you must do and cosmic power will always do its part. Flip the light switch by receiving new ideas. Cosmic power will then light up the mental room.

431. Q: We need more energy for acquiring self-wholeness.

A: A farmer owned a large field divided into two sections by an old and useless wall. But disliking the labor required to remove the wall, he continued to climb awkwardly over it several times a day. But he finally became so tired of the frustrating wall that he energetically knocked it down. In our lives, weariness over inner division arouses energy for ending it.

432.   Q: Please provide a tool for right inner work.
       A: If you look out a window at a certain angle it will appear that inside objects are outside the house. Reason tells you it is merely a reflection, that the objects are actually inside the room. Likewise, we think that negative attitudes are in other people, when they are really our own. Realization of this enables you to work in the right place for purification—within your own psychic system.

433.   Q: But suppose I see a negative attitude in another person. Where does that negative attitude reside?
       A: If you are unconsciously negative it resides in both you and the other person. If you are simply and clearly conscious of his negative state, it resides in him alone. But be very careful you do not project your own negative condition and believe that it exists only in the other person.

434.   Q: How can I test myself to see whether I am condemning others for the very negativities I conceal within myself?
       A: Notice how nervous and defensive you get when anyone comes close to whatever you are hiding.

435. Q: I have been accused of not having too much intelligence. What if it is true?

A: There is a totally new kind of intelligence which is above human judgments regarding intelligence. I will help you to start thinking about it. It is not intelligent to live in suppressed fear and hostility, yet millions of so-called intelligent people live with these terrors. Seek cosmic intelligence, for it answers all questions.

436. Q: Please comment on the acquisition of real strength.

A: A chief barrier to the acquisition of private strength is the wish to appear strong in public.

437. Q: It is the old story of preferring appearances over realities.

A: Imagine a hungry man who stands before an apple and a picture of an apple. He takes the picture. That is humanity.

438. Q: How does spiritual strength develop?

A: Strengthen what you can strengthen today, perhaps your reading of truthful books, and tomorrow you will be able to strengthen something else.

439. Q: I feel as if I'm living at the base of a smoldering volcano, about to erupt. What is this all about?

A: It is fear of yourself. You are beginning

to sense something that has been an unconscious fact up to now. You are seeing how little control you have of raging emotions. Have no fear, instead, begin to see through their false power.

440. Q: We are urged to honestly observe a negative fact about ourselves. How does this help?

A: An observed negative fact becomes a positive power. Never forget that. It is a fact that some parts of a man want nothing to do with self-transformation. The very realization of that fact aids self-transformation. By facing the illness, the doctor starts the cure.

441. Q: I need a second chance.

A: You can give it to yourself. Insight into your own cosmic resources gives you the second chance. This means you must look in a totally different direction than before. Let nothing distract you.

442. Q: What will we be able to do that we cannot now do?

A: You will be able to walk in and out of a new situation while remaining untouched by its negativities. You will be like a knight in armor who rides casually and unhurt through a forest of evil dragons. Most people walk into a new situation with bewilderment, remain in it with tension, and walk out with scars.

443. Q: I want to be more daring in this adventure.

A: Daring is doubled by being daring.

PROMINENT PRINCIPLES TO PONDER

a. Your cosmic nature is confidence itself.

b. Save energy by rejecting negative feelings.

c. Connect and use these ideas in every crisis.

d. Take the cosmic medicine and it will surely cure!

e. Our task is to let Reality replace imagination.

f. Do not permit other people to drain your energy.

g. Let your day belong to you, not to useless ideas.

h. You can make contact with cosmic command.

i. Self-responsibility attracts healing powers.

j. You can give yourself a new chance right now.

Chapter 8

ANSWERS TO BAFFLING QUESTIONS

444. Q: Why is it so hard to reach people with these ideas?

A:Anyone lacking cosmic knowledge does not know he lacks it. He will therefore reject information about its existence. Try to talk to a mule about music. Only a severe crisis can force him to seek something higher than his familiar but miserable world.

445. Q: Is this what you mean by using a crisis intelligently?

A: Using its humiliation to find a new life. The one way to win is to first come to that state of complete defeat in which the exhausted ego surrenders.

446. Q: It is clear that we must cease to feel offended when hearing what it is necessary to hear.

A: Feeling offended by cosmic fact is no different than a patient feeling resentful when the doctor offers the cure.

447. Q: We need help in distinguishing between wrong and right.

A: Then love truth above all else, for it alone will never betray you by saying that wrong is right.

448. Q: How can we choose right ways?

A: We can choose what is truly right for us only after a conscious effort to learn what is right and what is wrong, which means we must not assume we already know the difference.

449. Q: You have made it clear that truth resides beyond our own stubbornness.

A: Quite right. Once a seeker gets it through his head that he *cannot come to Truth on his own terms* he can come to Truth.

450. Q: We feel strongly about something and then feel the exact opposite an hour later. Why this contradiction?

A: Only insight into contradictory feelings can end them. Take a man who feels strong and confident when mingling with friends and crowds, but feels weak and lonely when returning home. He should realize that his confidence was false, for it was borrowed from a noisy atmosphere. True strength is independent of circumstances.

451. Q: Name a failure which blocks the cosmic highway.

A: Failure to see self-contradiction blocks self-freedom, as with the lecturer who was nervous over his forthcoming speech on the conquest of nervousness.

452. Q: Truth seems frightening at times but I do not understand why it should be. Please explain.

A: Truth is very frightening to who you are

not, but never to who you are in Reality.

453. Q: As a psychologist I notice how much people talk about former days, including childhood and happy or unhappy love affaires. How do you explain this?

A: Tied to time, they are unable as yet to be through with an event. They must learn what it means to sever the rope of time, to be finished with an event when it is finished. Cosmic consciousness dwells above time.

454. Q: I am often in carefully concealed anguish.

A: Anguish vanishes by realizing that something can appear important or even essential to one part of us while actually being as nothing to our real nature.

455. Q: To live from oneself sounds fascinating, but how is it accomplished?

A: A passenger was about to board an airplane when he was told he had too much luggage. He insisted upon taking everything with him—until seeing the error. Much of the baggage was not his own. The baggage of other passengers had been accidentally mixed with his possessions. On the cosmic flight we can happily leave all the burdensome ideas acquired from society. We need only what is truly our own.

456. Q: What is the difference between having a shallow moral code and having real spiritual rightness?

A: A man's moral code is the mask he puts on in the morning, while his spirituality is that tiny part that refuses to be fooled by it.

457. Q: How can we increase our appreciation of truth?

A: See what prevents it. A self-centered mind cannot appreciate truth. It is too busy worshipping itself. Can you think of anything more silly than worshipping a noise factory?

458. Q: A free man occupies a unique position. How did he get there?

A: A free man is where he is because of what he has done, such as entering and passing through dark tunnels within himself, which most people cannot even admit they have.

459. Q: When a seeker meets an awakened man, what happens?

A: Many interesting things. The seeker does not know at first that he is with an awakened man, for one can know in another only what he first knows in himself. The seeker will feel a crisis, for he must now decide whether to resist or learn the lessons. The awakened man knows all about the seeker, but will reveal his insight only as fast as the seeker can accept it.

460. Q: Revenge is wrong but is a popular practice. Why?

A: The moment of revenge supplies an

intense feeling of false pleasure. It seems to affirm the existence of the artificial self. Revenge, whether physical or mental, must obey the law of cause and effect by being followed by anguish and shame.

461. Q: Self-wholeness seems so distant.

A: A news story told about a detective who searched around the world for a lost relative. The missing man was finally located within ten blocks of the family which wanted to find him. We are very close to the enlightened person we wish to be but must realize it.

462. Q: When talking with someone, and trying to introduce these ideas, what should we remember?

A: That you are talking with a deeply confused human being who will fight with every fair and foul means the slightest suggestion that he is a deeply confused human being.

463. Q: What is an essential requirement for knowing the truth that sets us free?

A: Wanting it. Trying to give truth to those who don't want it is like trying to force a mule to appreciate a diamond.

464. Q: No doubt we accept substitutes for truth. Will you speak about this a bit?

A: Cleverness often passes for intelligence or spirituality. Charlatans easily fool most people with jokes and fancy phrases and dramatic manners. I will tell you what to do. The next time you are in serious trouble, go ask a charlatan to tell you a joke.

465. Q: Social schemes for human betterment end in failure in one way or another. Why?

A: For every person who is truly concerned for others there are a million people who wish to give the appearance of concern. Only a self-unified individual loves others.

466. Q: How can we improve society? Through organized protest against its evils?

A: You must rise to a certain level of insight toward society. You must see clearly that it does no good at all to angrily protest against society's evils. You might as well protest against a shark behaving like a shark. Society cannot change. *You* can change.

467. Q: Then why did Christ and Buddha and other great teachers preach to the masses?

A: So that the one man or woman in a thousand could hear and receive and understand and change.

468. Q: I wonder whether we have really loved anyone, or even know what it means to love.

A: The most loving act on earth is to diligently change one's inner nature so that one no longer unconsciously sends lies and cruelties into the world while calling them truths and benefits.

469. Q: What makes the world the mess that it is?

A: If everyone else in the world had the same internal state that you have, what kind of world would it be?

470. Q: Please explain a remark Jesus made to his disciples. He said he could not tell them many things because they would be unable to bear them.

A: If you only knew how few facts human beings can take. I will give you a small example of a fact people cannot face. People love to cry and moan, for it makes them the star of their own little egotistical stage performance. Now, suppose you give this fact to someone who is having the time of his life in weeping and moaning. You would arouse his hateful violence. See?

471. Q: When will we understand?

A: When someone asks you who you are, and you remain calmly silent, you understand.

472. Q: How can I know who I truly am?

A: You can know who you are by having the great courage and honesty of seeing who you are not. Do you know who you are not? You are not someone who needs to be concerned over who you are.

473. Q: It is obvious that stubborn self-will keeps us in the psychic jungle. What does it mean to do the will of heaven?

A: You do the will of heaven by *being* the

will of heaven. You become the will of heaven by giving up your wrong and unconscious assumption that you possess a separate and independent self. You then blend with heavenly will just as a small stream becomes part of a great river.

474. Q: We are beginning to see how society's weakness masquerades as strength. Please add to our insight.

A: Neurosis has incredible gall. Nothing can stop its destructive impudence. It behaves like a well-dressed goat who crashes into a party of birds with a brazen demand. It demands to be accepted as their teacher—in the art of flying!

475. Q: It is a common human trait to accuse others of having the very flaws we hide in ourselves.

A: A man who feared exposure by truth shouted angrily at the message of a real teacher. The angry man said that the teachings were nonsensical, cruel, confused. Afterward, the teacher was asked by his disciples, "Why did he describe truth like that?" Replied the teacher, "Because he did not know he was not describing truth at all, but was describing his own miserable condition."

476. Q: How does reward or punishment enter into all this?

A: A man is not rewarded or punished by what he does but by what he is; still, what he does is decided by what he is.

477. Q: A group of us were discussing the difference between an authentic teacher and a charming charlatan. We agreed that a real teacher supplies what is necessary, not what is soothing.

A: Correct. An enlightened person possesses a right kind of sternness which does not compromise with social deceit. It is really a compassionate sternness, an entirely different state than the self-centered sternness of neurosis.

478. Q: Why do nonsensical ideas draw huge audiences while truth-lectures often have few listeners?

A: Because human beings are more stimulated by crowds than they are attracted by truths.

479. Q: Nonsense is not only tolerated in this world but it is actually called creative intelligence.

A: Find an awakened man and you will be in one of those rare places where nonsense cannot enter.

480. Q: I would like to find an awakened man.

A: Then remember you cannot do so without first surrendering concealed guilt and vanity.

481. Q: I used to feel I was right about so many things which turned out all wrong. How was it possible to feel right and still be wrong?

A: Feeling right and being right can be two different things. A person can feel quite sure he can be told new things, but that is false rightness based on a mere image he has of himself as being receptive. The truth comes out when you try to give him new ideas, for then he gets nervous and defensive—which he never notices. When having cosmic facts you feel right calmly and permanently.

482. Q: We grope for solutions which elude us.

A: Like finding the key to the basement on the roof, the answer to every human problem is found in a psychic place which is higher than the problem.

483. Q: Why are we the victims of so many daily shocks, large and small?

A: Shock is a result of general unawareness of life and reality, like sleeping next to a dynamite factory. Your daydream expects one thing to happen, but something outside of that dream explodes instead.

484. Q: What is meant by our level of being?

A: Your level of being consists of your *actual* understanding of yourself and life. It is the fact of a man's condition as opposed to his flattering fantasies about himself. It does not consist of the way he appears to others, such as appearing wise and confident, but consists of the way he really feels toward himself in private. He must live with his own being, so is happy or unhappy according to its height or lack of height.

485. Q: How does his being affect his human relationships?

A: His level of being helps or harms himself and others equally. An impure river not only must live with itself but has no choice but to pass its impurity on to whatever it meets. So a person with a low level of being mechanically gives his harmful condition to others, though both he and the receivers may proudly believe that something noble and helpful is happening.

486. Q: I have a short question. Why are we lost?

A: We are lost in society's wilderness only because our weak psychic sight mistakes it for a rose garden.

487. Q: These teachings say that we cling to our suffering because it supplies a peculiar kind of pleasure. I find this hard to understand.

A: All right. Drop your suffering. Drop it right now and forever. Since this is possible to do, will you do it?

488. Q: I don't know.

A: You don't know because you have never tried it. Never having tried it you do not see how everything in you resists the dismissal of pain. You will do anything but give up your agony, for you enjoy its strange thrill. Try to see this.

489. Q: It would be pure magic if I could do it.

A: The ability to drop suffering the moment

it takes you over is one of the great psychic secrets available to sorrowful humanity. But there is even a higher level in which suffering cannot invade you in the first place.

490. Q: How do these principles explain human crime, such as violence and physical cruelty?

A: Crime is simply another result of man's immersion in psychic hypnosis. Every crime is a crime against the individual committing it, against his true interests. However, his own hardened beliefs prevent his awareness of this. His wrong attitudes must be melted down if he is to change from being his own worst enemy to being his own best friend.

491. Q: Where can I start being more self-honest?

A: See how scared you are.

492. Q: But that itself may scare me.

A: It cannot scare *you.* It can only scare the imaginary pictures you have about yourself, for example, the pictures you have of being calm and confident. Imaginary virtues always fear exposure.

493. Q: I have never admitted my greatest fear before, but this class has given me courage to come out with it. I fear being no one.

A: What! You fear being whole, healthy, happy? That is the result of being no one. To be no one simply means the absence of negativity, to not be the scared person you think and feel you are. You now feel yourself to be lost and helpless. There is a way to stop thinking that; there is a way to see that you are not your unhappy descriptions of yourself. Find that way, then see whether you still fear to be no one.

494.   Q: Who am I?

A: You are what you value—what you really value, not what you try to convince yourself that you value. If you value argument toward truth instead of receptivity you are an arguer and nothing else. If you value cosmic facts over society's schemes you are a sincere person in at least one way.

495.   Q: Can you tell me what I really value?

A: What kind of thoughts dominate your mind all day long? That is what you really value.

496.   Q: Please comment on miracles.

A: The disciples of an avatar pleaded with him to perform a miracle, to which he replied, "I will do even better than that. I will tell you how to perform your own miracles. A cosmic miracle happens when you become aware of an error *as* an error. The miracle is that it ceases to be an error."

497.   Q: Human beings think and talk and act around ideas of goodness, but goodness fails to appear. What goes wrong?

A: Who calls it goodness? What self-interest

lies behind it? A wolf's idea of goodness is to pounce on a sheep.

498. Q: What prevents us from being sincere students?

A: Many things, including laziness, self-pity, childish beliefs, a preference for social acceptance over individual wholeness. A compulsive talker who needs to convince you of how much he knows needs much more sincerity as a student.

499. Q: How can we invite right answers?

A: Remove your conditioned self out of the way. There is an answer to every question you may ask. It may not be the answer you want or expect, but it will be the cosmically correct answer. So do you want a vanity-pleasing wrong answer or a life-giving right answer?

500. Q: Why are we so reluctant to give up a wrong position, even while sensing how it injures us?

A: Because you identify with the position. This means that you take it as being yourself, which it is not. But having identified with a particular attitude or belief you now fear that its loss will cause you to lose what you call yourself. Your real nature does not consist of this or that position any more than you are the coat you put on and off. Your true self resides above all mental positions. Find it.

501. Q: You say that the end of one negative state tends to weaken another useless state. Example, please.

A: When we are not afraid we are also not hostile, for these two emotions go together, like two bad imps.

502. Q: Anger is such a constant problem with us.

A: Anger is an attempt to preserve the false self. Suppose a man is criticized or feels that other people are laughing at him. He reacts with anger at the feeling of loss to his so-called self-esteem. The thrill of anger seems to restore his feeling of worth. But it is all in vain, for there is no false self to protect. As a seeker sees this, his anger fades.

503. Q: What does inward success depend upon?

A: For one thing it depends upon whether you are willing to travel beyond familiar but useless sources of help to the Supreme Source.

504. Q: How can we find the Supreme Source?
A: Find yourself.

505. Q: What kind of change occurs in those who hear and apply these teachings?

A: One characteristic of those who are dropping their chains is their increasing fondness for self-honesty.

506. Q: What is meant by victory in defeat?
A: A man feared that truth wished to

destroy something of value within him. So day and night he battled and evaded truth. He even tried to twist truth into being what he wanted it to be, which left him tired and frustrated and defeated. But he finally saw that truth wished only to end everything worthless and anxious within him. As a new man he said to truth, "Thank you for not giving in to my immaturity."

REST UPON THESE RELIABLE TRUTHS

a. An exhausted self has a chance for self-newness.

b. Truth alone will never betray a man or woman.

c. We must come to Truth on the terms of Truth.

d. You need only what is truly your own.

e. Spiritual health is a result of self-honesty.

f. Sincerity will lead you to an authentic teacher.

g. Our insight determines the quality of our life.

h. No one is the scared person he imagines he is.

i. You are what you actually value inwardly.

j. True success comes by going beyond the familiar!

Chapter 9

HOW TO CHANGE WHO YOU ARE

507. Q: I wish to start life all over.

A: You can start life all over right now with a simple willingness to no longer be who you have always been.

508. Q: What is a requirement for self-newness?

A: A man must reach the point where he feels he must come back to himself, like a wandering child who knows he must return home before dark.

509. Q: Can I really change the kind of person I am?

A: Something that is not of your usual nature can change you, so give in to it with even an ounce of understanding, and more understanding and more change will come.

510. Q: I have asked myself a thousand times why I put up with my negative life, but have never heard an answer.

A: You put up with it because you fear its loss will leave you with nothing. I will tell you a tremendous secret. Leave yourself with nothing and you will have everything.

511. Q: Can I know that by personal experience?

A: You can know a thousand times more

about your life here on earth than you now know—so why delay your investigation?

512. Q: You are right about my fear of losing the familiar but false.

A: A loss of the false will be followed by a gain in the true. Strength replaces weakness, insight replaces ignorance, lightness replaces heaviness.

513. Q: How do we unknowingly block our own progress?

A: The last thing people want to do is to think in a new way. This is because their various self-labels, such as being a success or a failure, is made up of their old ways of thinking which they fear to drop.

514. Q: Are you saying that a man values the thought of being a failure?

A: Certainly. He would prefer to think of himself as a success, but if unsuccessful he will gladly label himself a failure, for he is at least someone who has failed. It is the self-reference which is falsely important to him, for he fears the lack of labels. A person will label himself almost anything to avoid facing the fact that his true nature needs no labels at all.

515. Q: Then thinking in a new way means to think without self-labels and self-reference?

A: Yes, which is the same as union with God, with Truth.

516. Q: These teachings can save anyone, yet a man or a woman continues to run wild. Why?

A: There is no way to get through to him. He does not even know there is no way to get through to him. His mind lacks the clarity to see even this elementary lesson. He fails to see himself as Reality sees him. He pictures himself as competent and commanding, while Reality sees him as the nervous victim of his own bluff. Reality can begin to penetrate his psychic armor only when his pain becomes unbearable.

517. Q: This raving world seems to smother my efforts at becoming inwardly new.

A: Never attribute power to noise and neurosis. They have none. Just as you can wear a new coat while walking down a familiar street, you can acquire a new nature while walking through the usual world.

518. Q: This new nature is superior to the frantic world?

A: Because its nature is totally different than that of the world. Learn to be your own inner commander and no exterior person or circumstance will ever be able to command you.

519. Q: We must awaken to something new, but how?

A: Remind yourself every day that *the chief obstacle to self-awakening is the wrong and the unconscious assumption that one is already awake.*

520. Q: These principles speak about a new kind of success, about inner success. I am not sure what is meant.

A: At the end of the day an esoteric student said to himself, "I succeeded just once in walking across the room consciously, instead of unconsciously and mechanically." That is new success.

521. Q: What are the signs of the dawning of a new life and a new intelligence?

A: There are many indications. You drop the need to anxiously explain yourself to others. You have no compulsive urge to prove yourself right or to defend your position. You have no apologetic spirit.

522. Q: We are told we must come to the end of ourselves. I have never understood this.

A: Who is the man who finds himself? He is the man who finally runs out of hiding places. There are hundreds of hiding places, including unconscious daydreaming, a craving to appear important, a belief in human heroes and authorities. Man is a desperate seeker who runs from cave to cave in the mountain, hoping that one of them will offer refuge from a stormy world. Only when he comes to an end of hiding places can the energy in his desperation be turned into energy for reaching the top of the mountain.

523. Q: How many people can achieve this real change?

A: How many people can see the difference between having religion and having rightness?

524. Q: How can we stop evading what must be faced?

A: Evasion is the enemy of self-wholeness. Among other things it is a refusal of esoteric education, a blaming of others for our griefs, a belief that so-called authorities can rescue us. Evasion is always unconscious. The evader fails to see what he is doing against himself. So awareness of evasion is an honest and healthy contribution to self-wholeness.

525. Q: I fear I may go wrong.

A: You will never go wrong by questioning your present beliefs about yourself and your life. Human beings go wrong only because of failure to ask probing questions.

526. Q: What kind of questions should we ask?

A: Ask why you cling to beliefs that lead nowhere. Ask why you endure life instead of living it. Ask why you yearn for something different but fear to claim it. These are healthy questions leading to self-newness.

527. Q: May we hear more about right aims?

A: Your aim is not to win acceptance from society but to awaken from the dream which you wrongly assume is an awakened state. Your goal is not to use cosmic principles for shallow rewards but to win the Real Reward. Your objective is not to correct the lives of other people but to see how unconscious thoughts distort your own life.

528. Q: Maybe I am too complicated to understand all this.

A: You need not complicate it. A pianist chooses the right notes to attain musical harmony. So must we choose the right cosmic principles to attain life-harmony.

529. Q: What makes self-transcendence possible?

A: Your ability to become acquainted with yourself in two different ways. First you become acquainted with your false self which consists of dreary outlooks, deceitful motives, feelings of superiority and so on. In other words you become acquainted with your present negative self. This arouses a deep urge to stop living as this kind of person, which causes negative traits to fall away. You then become acquainted with your real nature, which is self-transcendence.

530. Q: All of us have an uneasy feeling that we might be found out. Will you please discuss this?

A: We fear exposure only when hiding something. Innocence is fearless. A merchant complained of nervousness and irritability. A wise man told him, "Stop trying to pass off faulty merchandise as quality goods. No wonder you are anxious. You are in nervous fear of being found out." The merchant's nervousness vanished as he followed the wise man's advice.

531. Q: How do you define innocence?
A: A state of being who you really are.

532. Q: Over the years I have studied many spiritual books and practiced many disciplines, but feel unrewarded by heaven for all my hard work.
A: I know. You feel cheated by heaven. If you only knew how many people fall into this trap. I will explain the trap. You are trying to bargain with heaven, just as you agree to pay money in exchange for potatoes or paint. Heaven never bargains.

533. Q: But I don't think I am doing this.
A: Start thinking it. Just notice a certain kind of bitterness inside you which feels it has given so much and gained so little in return. Then see that bitterness toward heaven or toward other people has a false foundation which can be destroyed by pure understanding.

534. Q: No doubt you are right about my suppressed bitterness. It is a relief to face it.
A: Now proceed to dissolve it. A cosmically new nature has no connection with bitterness. A free bird soaring the sky never thinks of a cage.

535. Q: It is difficult to understand how a new nature can remain pure in this wicked world.
A: A magnificent ruby was carried through storms and heats and floods until reaching an emperor's palace. It remained a magnificent ruby

throughout the journey. Your new nature is not part of the impure world, and therefore remains untouched by it.

536.   Q: What action leads to self-newness?

A: Self-newness comes by deliberately plunging into the dark while fearing to do so. Plunging into the dark means to suspend habitual beliefs and reactions, which makes room for something truly new.

537.   Q: Why do we fear to do this?

A: Familiar thoughts and opinions seem to supply a feeling of security. Regardless of how often they spill us into the psychic swamp we prefer their familiarity over the true. You can plunge into the dark by seeing how your present ideas betray you, how they keep you tense and self-defensive. You will emerge from the dark with self-newness.

538.   Q: What new kind of success will arrive?

A: With calm command you will know what to do with yourself all day long.

539.   Q: I have a problem which is also a problem of several others in the group. I feel strained and drained by trying to be the kind of person that other people expect me to be.

A: Then feel relieved right now. Live up to what your own nature expects of you and you can forget about the expectations and demands of others.

146

540. Q: Give us something to do today.

A: Today, open one small psychic door to admit more spiritual light, and today will be one of the great days of your life.

541. Q: Give us a challenging fact to work upon.

A: You now lead imaginary lives, calling them real. Not only do you not realize this but you have no idea of how you fight every attempt to explain your condition to you. You fight because you fear the loss of your imaginary lives will spill you into chaos. Your lives are nothing but chaos right now, but rigid imagination prevents insight into this. Only the loss of your imaginary existence can open the gate to the real. Then you will return to your true nature.

542. Q: Can I really come back to myself?

A: Nothing prevents it but your own belief in blockage. Now, won't it be a positive pleasure to give up everything that stands in the way of your return?

543. Q: I am trying to understand, but need simplification. How can I become a new person?

A: Become new by not clinging to the acquired ideas of who you think you are. Ponder that single sentence.

544. Q: Can beneficial results be known in advance?

A: Right effort will certainly produce right

147

results. However, by trying to know them in advance you wrongly activate memory, which consists of the old and the familiar. When planning to visit a new country you do not imagine it to be the same as your homeland. Let the cosmic country reveal its newness as you travel along.

545. Q: What would you say to someone who believes that life is not worth living?

A: Anyone believing that life is not worth living should agree fully that it is meaningless *in its present form.* This is a truly positive attitude, for it drains away false mental guides and presents a drink of mental health. Out of this ego-defeat can arise New Life, which exists as surely as the sky.

546. Q: But what do we do?

A: What to do is very simple, but will you do it? Run the risk. That is what to do. Run the risk of being rejected, run the risk of being wrong, run the risk of being humiliated. Then when you are rejected or wrong or humiliated, take these feelings consciously. Repeatedly run the risk and you will run out of the jungle.

547. Q: You mean we should go against our usual behavior?

A: As often as possible. There is a special bonus in doing something for the first time, for you see how awkward you are. This is practical information you could not have had without the attempt. Correction is now possible. A man merely dreaming about finding a treasure never meets and conquers the obstacles blocking his discovery.

548. Q: Give us an obstacle to conquer.

A: A wish to be superior. Observe yourself right here in this class. Do you wish to be more spiritual, more attractive, more authoritative than others? Observe yourself with painful honesty. End that obstacle to real treasure.

549. Q: I see our problem. We say that we want self-newness but are unwilling to take the necessary action.

A: Thousands of people came to hear a message from a great teacher. Rich and poor, famous and unknown, all came to hear of the way to liberation. The teacher told them, "You wish liberty from your concealed anxiety? I will show you the way in a single sentence. Cease your secret plots against each other, for they are the same as plots against yourself. Now we will see how many of you really want self-liberty."

550. Q: Help us to find God.

A: Turning toward God without also turning away from mere beliefs about God is as impossible as walking and standing still at the same time.

551. Q: That is a new idea to me.
A: Let it make you new.

552. Q: Perhaps we should review elementary

lessons. What simple truth must we see more clearly?

A: Can you receive a real ruby into your hand while tightly clutching an artificial ruby inside your fist? No. To receive the real ruby you must first open your hand and drop the artificial gem. To obtain real life we must first detect and drop artificial ways.

553. Q: What prevents us from seeing things as they are?

A: Your wish to see things as you wish to see them. But since this is unconscious you will deny doing so.

554. Q: How can we create an opportunity for self-newness?

A: A person either gives himself his own opportunity or he rejects his opportunity. *It depends upon how much or how little he can be told about his actual condition.* The more he can be told the faster his mind and life rises. It is a tremendous talent to be able to be told about our actual condition. Develop this kind of talent.

555. Q: I sense that inner transformation is caused by thinking in a new way, but how does this new thinking become possible?

A: It is possible to think of life-changing ideas for the first time, provided we do not assume we already think them.

556. Q: Please mention a form of freedom from other people.

A: As a person becomes more responsible for his own actions he sees with relief that other people are also responsible for their own behavior.

557. Q: I believe you know a lot more about each of us than you reveal. I know we must be given small doses of medicine at a time, but maybe we can bear a larger dose.

A: What would happen if you discovered you were not at all the kind of person you take yourself to be? What if all your virtues proved to be imaginary? What if all your accomplishments proved to be worthless? Could you take it? Not at all. Not yet. You have no idea how your unconscious fears would fight the appearance of this discovery. Yet this discovery leads to wholeness.

558. Q: We need a new approach.

A: Instead of asking how you can become new, do something that will show you how.

559. Q: What might we do?

A: Place curing facts before pleasant fantasies.

560. Q: Then we need to know the difference between facts and fantasies. How can we distinguish?

A: The conditioned mind can never distinguish. Cease to take as true what you now assume is true. That faint and vague and mysterious yearning you have for a different kind of life is authentic, so listen to it, while ignoring all other voices which try to lead you astray.

561. Q: How can we see our real and truly valuable nature?

A: See through your artificial nature. Can't you feel that your surface personality is a tyrant? Can't you see how it pretends friendship while actually turning your hours into frantic scrambles for psychic survival? This insight removes a dragon blocking the road to Reality.

562. Q: We sense a need to be unique. I don't mean the vain uniqueness of having worldly fame and power, but of being free of inner tyrants.

A: Be the one person in a million who sees anger as a false form of pleasure which keeps the ego intact. This ego is the chief tyrant. Do this and you will be a truly unique person.

563. Q: I wish to understand true individuality.

A: Start by seeing the characteristics of false individuality. It must always be supported by other people and fears their disloyalty. It resents any suggestion that it is false. Its arrogance quickly turns to anxiety and then goes back to arrogance. It can have considerable exterior charm, while actually having contempt for others. True individuality is a result of Cosmic Oneness.

564. Q: Can anyone become a new kind of person?

A: Any human being can change who he is by first abandoning all unconscious images which falsely tell him who he is—but how many human beings are willing to go this far?

565. Q: We are reluctant to make right efforts.

A: How strange that we protest when asked to make an effort to collect inner riches. Complaining at the task of self-change is no different than complaining when told to go out and pick up diamonds!

566. Q: Give us something to shake us up, wake us up.

A: Each time you win something in this world you should bluntly ask yourself what you have really won, for that will open your eyes to a new kind of winning in a new kind of world.

567. Q: I have a multitude of questions but a scarcity of answers!

A: Any question you ask yourself can be answered by yourself, provided you let your new nature do the answering.

568. Q: You say we can make a right use or a wrong use of these principles. Please explain the difference.

A: Imagine a man who takes a stroll in the countryside because he enjoys the scenery of a beautiful lake and rolling hills and colorful flowers.

Imagine a second man who walks the countryside in order to impress other people with his acquired knowledge of the scenery. In your spiritual stroll, be like the first man, for a simple fondness for truth creates a new nature.

569. Q: I find these teachings increasingly charming.

A: Nothing is more charming than the cosmic message of self-newness. Do you see why? You *feel* its rightness.

PRACTICAL PLANS IN SUMMARY

a. A willingness to change begins the change.

b. Let truth replace heaviness with lightness.

c. Think of the beauty of thinking in a new way!

d. Never attribute power to discouraging ideas.

e. A wish to understand life attracts understanding.

f. Your aim is to win a new kind of success.

g. Right efforts always supply right results.

h. Self-investigation leads to self-wholeness.

i. Your real nature can answer every question.

j. The path is both practical and charming.

Chapter 10

PEARLS FOR YOUR COSMIC TREASURY

570. Q: I am pleased at the way these teachings never dodge complex questions, but answer them simply and accurately, without fear of offending listeners. Other teachings cannot do this.

A: This simplicity and directness are characteristic of the man who really knows the way out of the human swamp.

571. Q: In my efforts to rescue myself I have tried dozens of philosophies and beliefs. None have helped. I feel like a weary ship unable to find a friendly harbor.

A: Congratulations. When your despair reaches the breaking point, come see me again. I have good news for you about a totally different kind of harbor.

572. Q: May I have a hint about its nature?

A: It is not made up of memory or of imagination.

573. Q: In trying to comprehend all this I find my mind turning in repetitious circles.

A: Simply remember that the ordinary mind cannot comprehend these higher facts. This remembrance prevents you from trying to fly on a bicycle. This clarity can now begin to help you fly with Cosmic Consciousness, which comprehends everything.

574. Q: We try to convince ourselves we are winning, but something within knows we are losing.

A: So change it. Your real nature can never lose when you are with an authentic teacher. It always wins something informative and inspiring.

575. Q: An authentic teacher?

A: A true teacher can be a person who has transcended ordinary life or can be your own released Cosmic Intelligence. An authentic teacher can help you find your Cosmic Intelligence and your Cosmic Intelligence can help you find an authentic teacher.

576. Q: It seems we are failing to pay attention.

A: Imagine a sea captain strolling along the shore. He observes some people having a wild party on a boat a short distance out to sea. Seeing that a storm is about to break he tries to signal the people to return to harbor, but they are too busy having fun to pay attention. So they are caught in the storm. The signal for humanity's safety can be seen, but few are paying attention.

577. Q: Does science enter into these studies?

A: A scientific question that can carry you toward real success is, "What is happening within me at this present moment?"

578. Q: We need something to shake us out of our psychic sleep. What can awaken us?

A: Suppose a man declares his intention

of walking north, but mistakenly starts toward the south. You try to correct him, but his stunned pride refuses to listen. What can shock him into wanting to correct himself? Only an honest facing of the deception and the desolation of his wrong course. Try to see into the depths of this explanation. It can start self-awakening.

579. Q: Help us to understand ourselves.

A: Look at any human being. Know for sure that the invisible person is totally different from the visible person. The person who *thinks* is different from the person who *speaks*. The person who *feels* in a certain way will *act* in a totally different way. This is a painful and unnecessary state of self-division. Seek singleness.

580. Q: Please review our purpose in applying these ideas.

A: To state it one way, the purpose is to change our internal geographic location. Men and women live in deserts of mental worry and irritability. They flounder around in swamps of emotional chaos. That is the internal geographic location of most people. You need not remain like most people.

581. Q: Why is Reality rejected?

A: Lovers of delusion dislike anything which is unlike delusion. And the thing most unlike delusion is Reality. To make his disciples wise when teaching truth in a deluded world a teacher told them, "Never offer cabbage to a man who dislikes cabbage."

582. Q: But if enough people organize to make this a better world it will surely produce a good result.

A: A million sheep who organize in the belief that they are conscious human beings are still a million sheep.

583. Q: How can we escape society's net of delusion?

A: Start by seeing very clearly and very deeply that all man-made systems for human improvement are pathetic attempts to make nothing look like something.

584. Q: So the enemy is unseen egotism?

A: Imagine a country terrorized by an unseen but powerful dictator. He ruins lives, causes heartache, spreads lies and confusions. Here we have the perfect picture of the tyranny of unconscious egotism. Terrorized people are those who fail to overthrow the tyranny of egotism. As aid in overthrowing it, remember that egotism never calls itself egotism, but masquerades as various forms of goodness.

585. Q: How can we protect ourselves in a malicious world?

A: See things as they are. You are then like a traveler who walks safely through a perilous jungle, protected by his very knowledge of its dangers.

586. Q: How can I start a fresh flow of energy?
     A: Energy starts to flow the moment you place your attention on something. Placing your attention on ways to outwit other people or on defending errors is a dreadful waste of natural energy. But placing attention on ways to banish the bluff of depression is both highly intelligent and productive. Where is your attention all day long?

587. Q: You have made me think about it.
     A: Something truly good will come from it.

588. Q: I hope this is not an odd question, but if I could live today over, could I make it different?
     A: You would make the same mistakes, have the same inner arguments, end up at the same places.

589. Q: But why?
     A: Because any machine, whether an automobile or a human machine can only repeat its own mechanical nature.

590. Q: Then how can tomorrow be different?
     A: By being a conscious human being today.

591. Q: I don't understand why everything remains the same—the same bewilderments, the same hidden aches.

A: A woman walked up to the third floor of an office building, seeking a dealer in rare coins. She was puzzled at her inability to find the shop. Reviewing the address she carried, she saw her mistake. She had to go higher—to the sixth floor where the dealer was located. Remember the law of levels. Cosmic law decrees we must make an inward ascent in order to find the rare life we really want.

592. Q: We may put on cheerful faces, but most of us feel surrounded by an invisible wall.

A: Every bit of welcomed truth makes another crack in the psychic wall which will finally collapse to reveal the New World beyond.

593. Q: Why is worry so hard to abolish?

A: Because it is very clever in disguising itself as necessary, as essential to psychic survival. Oddly, worry supplies a feeling of self-importance, making us feel as if great and exciting things are happening to us. This is nothing masquerading as something. Begin to see that worry is not necessary to your real nature.

594. Q: What is true gentleness?

A: True gentleness is real strength. Only a real person can express gentleness, for it appears in the absence of artificiality and insolence. Gentleness cannot be understood nor taken rightly by anyone lacking gentleness within himself. He will distort it, calling it weakness. His idea of gentleness is a sentimental stage performance from which he hopes to gain some kind of advantage.

595. Q: Someone says things that upset me. How can I get him to stop?

A: Never mind what he says. What do you feel? Why are you a slave to hurt feelings? He sees your distress as a handy target for his own pressures. Work with these ideas until you disappear as a target. He will disappear as an archer.

596. Q: Let me state it as simply as possible. I want my life to be right.

A: A part of you *is* right, but you do not as yet know which part it is. It is like having a single diamond mixed up with fifty glass stones. Classwork shows you how to detect and isolate the diamond.

597. Q: Let me see whether I understand. I have a right part? What is it? How can it be detected and separated from the glass stones?

A: The right part itself will help you in its own unique way. It will help by enabling you to recognize glass stones when you see them. When knowing glass and rejecting it the diamond is then recognized as being something different.

598. Q: I think I see. Are you saying that the glass stones are the artificial parts of human personality, such as impudence and harshness?

A: The glass stones are anything which prevents us from recognizing the diamond.

599. Q: I want to work twice as hard to understand this.

A: Then work twice as hard at calling glass stones exactly what they are—glass stones.

600. Q: Where might we start on this new course?

A: Let the outer man become acquainted with the inner man.

601. Q: How can we escape the psychic cave?

A: Stop calling the cave a castle. You do this but are unaware of it. You call the cave a castle because you fear there may not be a real castle out there in the sunshine. There is a real castle, but your resistance to truth keeps you in the cave which is called a castle.

602. Q: Several of us ride together to these meetings. May we have a topic for discussion on the way home?

A: Light loves more light. Darkness loves more darkness.

603. Q: Higher teachings state that we refuse to hear the blunt facts which could start the cure. What is an instance of this?

A: The vast majority of human beings live in artificial concern for others. This is the last thing that artificial people want to hear.

604. Q: Do you mean that our apparent concern for others is actually self-concern in disguise?

A: That is one way to state it. Real concern for others cannot be separated from real concern for your own inner wholeness. Therefore, the only way to develop an authentic conscience is to be rightly concerned with obtaining your own cosmic health. That health will then radiate itself generously, naturally, and without thought, to all those who want health for themselves.

605. Q: I feel that I am at the mercy of everyone, including myself.

A: Try to see that your life is *your* life which need not be sacrificed to false ambitions or to cunning charlatans.

606. Q: Personal problems seem too hard for my mind to solve.

A: Any problem can be solved by thinking about it in the right way, the right way being cosmic in nature, far above one's present way. Your mind can rise to this lofty level.

607. Q: Where does help from others rightly end and self-help begin?

A: Another person cannot prove to you the effectiveness of these ideas, but you can prove them to yourself, just as you personally prove the flavor of a peach.

608. Q: Since we are with ourselves all day long, we must learn to be self-teachers.

A: Every thought and feeling and action is a

teacher. So what are you teaching yourself all day long? Examine it. Each time you permit a thought of defeat you teach yourself to be increasingly defeated. Each time you feel the need for a different way to live you teach yourself facts for accomplishing this.

609. Q: Then our emotions are teachers also?

A: Feelings have extraordinary power to instruct. Take someone who feels that his life is not really going anywhere. He has enough money, has many friends and exciting involvements, yet feels he always returns to the same empty place within himself. Consciousness of that feeling can turn him in a new direction.

610. Q: I don't know where these truths are taking me.

A: Great! Remain in that state. Don't ask why. Just remain in that state. You will see!

611. Q: You gave us an assignment of studying human faces. I learned many things, for example, human faces are great actors and actresses.

A: Yes, they are great performers in producing the desired effect on the audience, that is, on other people. A face can express pleasantness, confidence, wisdom, compassion, authority, friendliness—all stage performances. But actors and actresses are always fearful that others might see through their performances.

612. Q: Where do the masses of people go wrong in thinking about God and spirituality?

A: The great blunder made by humanity is to believe that a mere *idea* about God or goodness is the same as God or goodness.

613. Q: We change our minds a dozen times a day, often switching to an opposite position. I am puzzled at how fickle we are.

A: Are you puzzled when a scared rabbit darts off in every direction? A rabbit has no psychic unity. Neither has man. He is one person in the morning, another at noon, and a third kind of person at night, never noticing his contradictions. Now you know why self-unity is an important aim in this class.

614. Q: I sense the rightness of a certain procedure followed in this class. We never waste time discussing weird or merely sensational topics. They have nothing to contribute toward making us whole and sensible human beings.

A: Right. Why play with toys when medicine is needed?

615. Q: How are we tricked and injured by delusion?

A: In hundreds of ways. For example, can you see that emotional exhilaration is not the same as lasting happiness? Think about that.

616. Q: You once urged us to question our lives.

It is a bit disturbing at first, but I see its value.

A: Man is like a stranded tourist who endlessly boards wrong ships because he never asks questions about their destinations.

617. Q: So let me ask about something that has baffled me for a long time. Since there is a way to attain inner peace, why do so few find it?

A: People actually love their inner warfare, for it provides a thrilling distraction from doing the one thing they fear most of all—honest self-facing.

618. Q: We reject what we should accept, and accept what we should reject!

A: The healing truth can be compared with a new kind of cosmic medicine given to the world by healthy human beings. But because it is unfamiliar to people, because it is unlike their usual medicines —which do not work anyway—they reject it. The healed are those who welcome, taste, and finally consume the cosmic medicine.

619. Q: We claim self-knowledge, but I wonder whether we have even tiny self-insights.

A: Lost people feel insulted when told they do not understand themselves, but that is precisely what they must admit if they are ever to find themselves.

620. Q: So we must act against our own vanity and act for our own self-knowledge.

A: Spiritual hunger can arouse right action

in acquiring self-knowledge, just as a hungry farmer walks toward his fruit trees.

621. Q: I used to value argument, thinking it indicated loyalty to principles. I look forward to overcoming other foolish notions.

A: In ancient India, two teachers lived at opposite sides of a village. One day both teachers were challenged by members of a noisy religious sect. The visitors told each teacher, "Your ideas are false, while ours are true." The first teacher responded with angry argument. The second teacher listened with calm attention, not saying a word. The question is, which teacher was a true teacher?

622. Q: I have told you several things about myself, and no doubt you have observed much more. What specific advice can you give me?

A: See the fading of your fantasies as your opportunity for wholeness, not as your terror.

623. Q: Each time I think I have found a safe harbor it eventually turns into another stormy sea.

A: This is because you have an *idea* of the nature of the harbor. For example you have the idea that the harbor consists of a new marriage or a different place of residence or an excitement of some kind. The real harbor is Cosmic Consciousness, which is not merely an idea but a total Reality.

624. Q: But if it is not an idea, what is it?

A: It is that Supreme State which is irreplaceable. A mere idea is replaceable, as when you switch from an ambition to win empty public honors, to win what a foolish society calls spirituality. For now, try to see that Cosmic Consciousness is *not an idea of any kind.*

625. Q: What is inner transformation like?

A: Like bringing lighted lamps into the dark rooms of a mansion until everything is bright and clear.

626. Q: So our task is to see what can be seen?

A: An ancient myth told of a trail that ran through a valley. On one side was a mountain of glittering gold, while on the other side was a peaceful land of green grass and quiet streams. Travelers on the trail yearned for the quiet land, but did not see it. Their gaze was captured by the glittering mountain of gold. We can change the direction of our gaze.

627. Q: Suppose a man does not understand either himself or life, but assumes that he does. How can he begin to notice his self-contradiction?

A: He can notice how he gets fearful and angry when told that he does not really understand.

628. Q: My world shakes and shivers!

A: When you are right your world cannot be shaken, for your rightness is its own unshakeable world.

629. Q: But I don't know what it means to be right.

A: Eventually you will. A persistent preference for rightness over wrongness is half the victory. A small part of you wants what is right. With these studies you can make it the overwhelming power.

630. Q: Our failure to value the valuable is obvious.

A: Some people would be horrified at having an untidy home. The same people do not give the slightest attention to the disorder of their own minds.

631. Q: Why this neglect?

A: Because of the horrifying human talent for calling disorder order.

632. Q: What is the connection between earthly rewards and a truly spiritual existence?

A: There is no real connection. A public reputation for goodness is not connected with personal decency. Money is not related to inner wholeness. Being applauded as a scholar is not connected with cosmic intelligence.

633. Q: Give us something to correct our thinking.

A: A false assumption which serves self-interest will always be called a fact, which is as risky as calling a wolf a dog.

634. Q: We need to see the pleasantness of recovering our original nature.

A: While exploring an abandoned chapel in the hills of Wales, a naturalist found an old manuscript of music. Busy with his studies, he set it aside on a shelf in his home. Months later, curiosity led him to pick out the manuscript's notes on a piano. He heard a pleasing melody. Recovered truth has a pleasant and unique melody.

BE RECEPTIVE TO THESE GUIDES

a. Cosmic knowledge is your perfect protection.

b. You can uplift tomorrow by uplifting today.

c. When you change, everything changes!

d. Worry is not a part of your real nature.

e. Cosmic health radiates itself effortlessly.

f. Teach yourself this new way of daily victory.

g. The wise person replaces toys with medicines.

h. Your own lighted lamp makes everything clear.

i. An orderly mind is a powerful instrument.

j. Listen to the pleasant melody of cosmic facts.

Chapter 11

BE SECURE IN AN ANXIOUS WORLD

635. Q: Why do I fail in my plans to feel secure?

A: The best way to feel insecure is to have ideas as to what will make you feel secure. You have an idea that money or power or friendship will make you feel safe. It is the very thing that makes you unsafe, for ideas change, leaving you wondering what new idea to grab next.

636. Q: But what else is there?

A: There is something above ideas. That is all I want you to ponder for now. There is something above ideas.

637. Q: What we call good news either turns bad or we fear it may not last. Strange good news!

A: This world can no more produce good news than an oak can produce peaches. Authentic good news can come only from a totally different world, the invisible one. I am not speaking dramatically or sentimentally but factually.

638. Q: Please say more.

A: I will repeat the same good news in different words. A new world exists for you. Concealed desperation can end. There is a way out. You need not remain as you are. A new life can appear. Could you want greater good news?

639. Q: Why do we feel as if we are always on trial in a courtroom, submitting to accusation, examination, condemnation?

A: The courtroom exists only in your wrongly functioning mind. You may be convinced that it exists outside of you, but that is an error. You can walk out the moment you see that the courtroom doors have no locks. So walk out now. But I must add something. You will see your own liberty only when you no longer want to haul anyone else into court.

640. Q: What are we trying to do with all this?

A: We are trying to destroy something harmful. Start succeeding by seeing that the harmful always masquerades as the beneficial. Have you ever believed it necessary to pretend to understand something that really baffled you? That is harmful masquerade. Both the error and correction take place within your own mind.

641. Q: I wish my circumstances to be right.

A: When you are all right, everything else is all right.

642. Q: I am sure that each of us is his own worst enemy. May we hear of corrective action?

A: A story was written about a cruel conqueror who invaded an innocent country. The citizens were forced to huddle in front of him while he shouted at them with gleeful contempt. So intensely did he enjoy his sick screams that he failed to notice a nearby pit, into which he fell. Reckless attitudes are like that. They rob us of self-protective intelligence.

643. Q: How does spiritual knowledge help?

A: It is a first step toward enlightening experiences. You now have the knowledge that a troublesome person cannot cause trouble to your real self, to your awakened nature. Fine. Go on from there by bringing this knowledge into your daily contacts with people. One day you will *be* your knowledge, and therefore be untroubled.

644. Q: When will we have order in a disorderly world?

A: When everyone sees himself as the cause of the disorder. How many people do you know who want to see this?

645. Q: Help our studies to proceed in an orderly manner.

A: Make an aim to see and to be. You must first see in order to be. Seeing is on the level of ordinary thought, as when you observe a lack of self-resourcefulness. Being self-resourceful is the next orderly step, a result of higher consciousness which itself is a result of constantly throwing yourself back on yourself.

646. Q: Outwardly I may appear confident, but I am really terribly afraid of losing what I have.

A: If your earthly castle is shaking terribly

you should let it shake all it wants until it collapses completely. Then you can build the Cosmic Castle which cannot be shaken.

647. Q: Last week you told us about someone who achieved inner success. How did he start?

A: He resisted these teachings until something finally dawned on him. He realized he had to choose them or would remain like the rest of the world. He would have to remain tense and confused, covering up with nervous bluff. Realizing this, his decision was easy.

648. Q: My many activities fail to cure my insecurity.

A: A desperate feeling of insecurity is not cured by running out and doing things. If this could have cured insecurity it would have done so, for this is what most people do for most of the day, unconsciously of course. Then what can be done? Instead of chasing around like scared rabbits we can stay home mentally and do something truly wise. We can see that our real nature cannot feel insecure any more than an oak can feel angry words.

649. Q: Why do many religious activities fail to create anything real?

A: The memorizing of religious or philosophical ideas does not change a man's basic nature. He merely piles words on top of a pile of weaknesses. Believing that a man with a religious code is a decent man is like believing that a monkey with a trombone is a musician.

650. Q: Sometimes I wonder how I can ever handle all my problems.

A: Some day you will wonder how they ever could have affected you.

651. Q: Please discuss the difference between saying and doing.

A: Many people say they want to change themselves. Few really mean it. Most people have no intention of giving up their false pleasures derived from making demands, from appearing important, from feeling sorry for themselves. Tell someone he must give up such things and then see whether he really wants to change.

652. Q: What must we do to really change?

A: You must see as false what you now believe is true and see as true what you now take as false.

653. Q: In what specific ways?

A: You may now take it as true that other people must give in to your demands for more money, more love, more cooperation, more of anything else. This means you think the world revolves or should revolve around you personally. Since so many think this, society is the horror that it is. Stop thinking this.

654. Q: And what do we think is false which must be seen as true?

A: As one example, you may think it false that a higher way of life exists on this earth. It does exist, but ordinary viewpoints cannot see it any more than a fish can see the sun. Stop believing that your present life is the only life possible for you.

655. Q: Who is the devil?

A: The devil is simply the personification of everything wrong with human beings. The devil is therefore malice, hypocrisy, violence, cruelty, deception, ignorance and unconscious behavior. The devil in man never sees himself as a devil, in fact, he calls himself humble, religious, faithful and intelligent in an effort to convince himself and others that he is practically an angel on earth.

656. Q: I like the courage of these teachings. They are not afraid to see society as it actually is beneath surface appearances. Take away the false smiles and you have a rude and hostile world.

A: One of our liberties is to experience society's rudeness and hostility without permitting these unhealthy states to enter and injure us. They enter only when we are asleep at the gate.

657. Q: How can we reply to such a demanding society?

A: One day you will see something magnificent. You will see that you have nothing to say to

176

a neurotic world. You have no need to reply to its arrogant demands and accusations. Why do you have nothing to say? Simply because you know the truth that makes you free. Does a visitor in a zoo scream back at the howls from behind the bars?

658.　Q: Help us to realize what we are trying to do.

A: You need not complicate it with tumbling words. You are trying to turn inward night into day. You know what that means. Keep it as simple as that.

659.　Q: How do we see ourselves and the world wrongly?

A: Imagine yourself looking out a window to see a tree and the sky above it. Do you believe that the tree lives in a different world than the other trees you do not see? Do you think that the observed section of sky is apart from the rest of the sky? Our faulty psychic sight makes us believe we are separate from the All, when in fact we are included in the All.

660.　Q: What can help us transform our minds?

A: Do you think that habitual thoughts will tolerate your attempt to replace them with higher thoughts? Not at all. They will fight and scream and deceive in every possible way to continue to enslave you. But let this insight into their hostile nature help you conquer them. Insight is strength.

661. Q: By reversing the mind we also reverse results in the exterior world?

A: The one sure way to reverse results is to reverse your inner nature, which includes thoughts, emotions, reactions, goals, and so on. Take the idea of security. People anxiously seek security by attaching themselves to human organizations. That is as useless as seeking a king's crown in a den of foxes, but people cling to the error. Reverse it by seeking your crown in your own inner kingdom.

662. Q: Strong emotions carry me away from myself.

A: A flood carried a man's home away three times. He finally had sense enough to move away from the raging river. Be aware of your psychic location. If not liking it, use these lessons to move away.

663. Q: What do you mean by a false and unnecessary emotion?

A: Any negative emotion is false and unnecessary, including painful doubt and fearful imagination. They are unnecessary because they are not based on the realities of your existence. Negativity cannot occupy the cosmic castle of your real nature.

664. Q: Please supply a method for conquering fear.

A: Always go against your fear. For instance,

some people want to break out of themselves but are afraid to try. Just try. Go against your fear by listening to spiritual truths which make you afraid. I repeat, listen to the very cosmic facts which arouse fear. This is a great secret for the conquest of fear, known by conquerors.

665. Q: I am especially fond of one idea you gave us. You urged us to call the bluff on secret anguish. I like the idea of calling its bluff.

A: Anguish is like a fierce-looking but weak ghost who runs away the moment you make it clear you will not tolerate it.

666. Q: I feel anxious when I am misunderstood.

A: If a thousand people misunderstand you, but you really understand yourself, where is the problem?

667. Q: I think most people have a repressed complaint. They complain that they must perform the same boring duties every day, must cover the same tiresome ground. What is the answer?

A: Like an airplane capable of long flights, a new mind can carry you far beyond your present repetitious territory. That cosmic flight ends all complaint.

668. Q: I am attracted to the inner adventure, but need most of my time and energy for getting along in the social world.

A: Everytime you dare to do something for

your inner self instead of something for your social self you teach the social self how to act logically and happily in the outer world.

669. Q: You mean we will respond rightly in all circumstances?

A: To respond rightly to a circumstance we must see it wholly, without the interference of self-centered thought, like a doctor who understands both the cause and cure of an illness.

670. Q: What particular circumstance might we see wholly?

A: Be aware of how people try to make you feel guilty over living your own life, then refuse it.

671. Q: May we have a guide for avoiding traps set for us by individuals and organizations?

A: When someone tells you the reason he does something, try to find the real reason.

672. Q: A menacing world makes us anxious. Can that be corrected?

A: The escape you want from a menacing world is as close as your own mind. This does not mean to retreat from the world, but to let cosmic wisdom lift you above it. Protection from the human battle does not come by trying to win, but by living above the battlefield.

673. Q: How does this connect with handling daily events?

A: As you begin to handle daily events consciously, with higher understanding, you accomplish two things for yourself. You turn the events from enemies into friends, and you prevent negative events from happening in the first place. This is a marvelous way to live. You can live this way.

674. Q: I really don't know how I am supposed to behave in society.

A: Put it another way. You are not obligated to behave like a nitwit just because millions of others do.

675. Q: But what do I owe others?

A: Just one thing. A sane mind.

676. Q: I have a full share of problems with people. What kind of self-examination can help?

A: Ask yourself where you might be gullible toward people without realizing it.

677. Q: You say we must do first things first. In what area, for example?

A: To live under the freedom of his cosmic nature a man must first see that he is presently living under the tyranny of his stubborn likes and dislikes.

678. Q: It is shocking to hear that I am living under the tyranny of my own negative nature, but I sense it as a fact. What next?

A: Realize the enormous profit in studying and finally ending unconscious self-contradictions.

679. Q: I can see why self-study is essential.

A: Trying to understand life without a deep study of oneself is like trying to comprehend a book without reading it. In time you will be able to read yourself like a book. At that point the real motives and cunnings of other people become clear to you, which is protection.

680. Q: So we must start doing things truly favorable for ourselves?

A: Yes, but first you must discover the difference between doing something for yourself and doing something for false personality. What is the good in giving cosmic gold to a dreamer who can't value it?

681. Q: How can we discover whether or not we are impractical dreamers?

A: What is your day like? You are a dreamer to the degree that your day is filled with tension and uncertainty.

682. Q: I have just read the idea that a man *gets* what he *is*. What does that mean?

A: An imp felt mistreated by other imps with whom he associated. He felt slandered and betrayed and hurt. Meeting an angel the imp complained, "I wish only good for others, but look what they do to me." The angel sighed,

"You imps never learn. When associating with evil imps you are simply associating with your own nature. What on earth do you expect?"

683. Q: A member of this class helped me with a casual remark. She said that we are in danger only from ourselves. May we have your ideas on this?

A: A man is endangered only by his own delusions which he has carefully concealed from himself. He can be saved only by his own real virtues which are hidden from view by the walls of delusion. We are safe only on the other side of the wall. Will you climb it?

684. Q: We are defeated by our lack of self-knowledge. I never saw it that way before.

A: Take the demand of wanting our own way. We all want our own way but don't want the consequences. That is no different than demanding a cup of salty sea water and then demanding that it taste like fresh water. See how self-knowledge can end disastrous consequences?

685. Q: Why is it wrong to accept authority in spiritual matters?

A: How do you know whether or not the authority really knows what he is talking about? Maybe your own insecurity has frantically erected a false idol. Also, when accepting something from authority you leave your own intelligence out of it. Is that intelligent? People find it very easy to abandon an authority when seeing a personal advantage in doing so.

686. Q: Then how can we relate to a real teacher?

A: At a certain point in your own inner development you will know whether or not another person speaks the truth. At this point it is safe and helpful to listen to him.

687. Q: Please explain the difference between a conscious man and a man still in delusion.

A: The difference between the spiritually awakened man and the unenlightened man is this: The unawakened man denies the existence of psychic tigers and foxes within himself. Outwardly he may appear humble and innocent, but he is still part of the psychic jungle. The awakened man has bravely entered the self-jungle and has conquered the wild beasts. You can see why the conscious man is fearless, while the unawakened man is still afraid.

688. Q: Then an awakened man is free from society while living in the midst of it?

A: Society has as much to give to an awakened man as a single word has to give to a dictionary.

689. Q: The desire for social success has twisted us out of psychic shape. How can we relax into normality?

A: Cosmic Consciousness does not see any difference between a social success and a nobody. Only human carelessness thinks it sees a difference. Uplift your mind to where you no longer see a difference, for then you will have a new kind of success unknown by senseless society.

690. Q: Why are delusions so powerfully persistent?

A: When a frantic man believes that his psychic security requires two and two to add up to five, the greatest mathematician on earth will be unable to convince him otherwise.

691. Q: Why are we so tyrannized by anxiety?

A: Because anxious thoughts trick us into believing they are necessary. They are about as necessary as rocks on the dinner table. As an example, it is unnecessary to anxiously think that happiness depends upon the loyalty of friends.

692. Q: How does happiness connect with viewpoints?

A: In Brazil there is a stream with a curious feature. It appears to be running uphill—but only when viewed from a certain spot. Close inspection shows it to be running normally downhill. When life is seen from the viewpoint of worldly success we seem to ascend in happiness. It is a deceptive viewpoint. Happiness is a state in which life is seen as it is in reality.

693. Q: This helps me understand what life is all about.

A: You are engaged in the pleasant task of exchanging pebbles for pearls.

694. Q: I am afraid we live in a world of fear.

A: People go through life pleading, "Please don't scare me." You must do much better. You must proceed differently. You must state to a teacher of truth, "Go ahead and scare me if necessary, for I will use it to awaken from the nightmare."

695. Q: By intelligently using a negative condition we can end it. That is a fascinating idea.

A: It proves that real intelligence conquers all.

FOLLOW THESE USEFUL INSTRUCTIONS

a. Good news comes only from the cosmic world.

b. With self-insight you can walk away from anxiety.

c. The harmful often disguises itself as the good.

d. Cosmic wisdom dares to see things as they are.

e. Ignore unhealthy demands from other people.

f. Your simple goal is to turn night into day.

g. If not liking your psychic location, move away!

h. Learn to call the bluff on suppressed anguish.

i. You are now doing favorable things for yourself.

j. A conscious individual is bold and fearless.

Chapter 12

BOLDLY VENTURE AND CONQUER

696. Q: About a month ago you spoke about an invisible miracle. What did you mean?

A: Most people let visible conditions dictate their invisible states, as when people get scared and gloomy over bad economic news. You can be different. Through cosmic insight your invisible states can be right regardless of visible conditions. This is an invisible miracle.

697. Q: I *know* more than I can *do*!

A: I am glad you realize it. You can *know* an idea for years and still be unable to use it for daily benefit. In this class we are learning to *live* what we *know*. Take the idea that painful feelings cannot enter a conscious mind. You can know this as an idea and still get your feelings hurt. We have much to do, so let's get busy!

698. Q: Thanks to these teachings I am seeing the need for detecting and abandoning wrong attitudes.

A: Departing from a wrong attitude is as intelligent as jumping off a runaway train before it crashes. Jump.

699. Q: What is inspiration?

A: There is false inspiration based on unseen vanity and there is constructive inspiration based on cosmic consciousness. I will tell you how to live in healthy inspiration. Constantly choose the right instead of the thrilling. You will eventually see the difference between artificial and authentic inspiration, and will want only the authentic.

700. Q: How can we see what is on top of the mountain?

A: See thoroughly the nature of the prairie. See its dryness, its emptiness. The prairie must first be understood because you must travel across it on the way to the mountain.

701. Q: You mean we must see our inner desolation?

A: See it without despair. See it with the intention of crossing the prairie to reach the mountain.

702. Q: Self-knowledge is essential, but the method eludes me.

A: You understand your own nature by observing every thought and action, just as a bird is understood with daily watchfulness.

703. Q: Please say more about right encouragement.

A: Authentic encouragement is to tell someone the whole truth about his life here on earth. For example, he can be told that he is a problem to himself, but a problem which can be solved.

704. Q: How does this help?

A: It helps because it is the truth itself, because it is the fact which can arouse right action toward self-rescue. It will help if you understand false encouragement. An example of this is to urge someone to seek self-fulfillment through fame and power. This is false advice because it can lead only to inner emptiness, regardless of success in society.

705. Q: Then it is right self-encouragement to really see the folly of seeking public prizes.

A: Public prizes can't contribute to the wholeness of the secret life any more than a log can contribute fruit.

706. Q: Then the only person capable of supplying authenic encouragement is someone who has truly found himself?

A: Exactly. Such a man achieves something very rare in this world—the ability to tell the truth.

707. Q: What prevents us from winning inner wealth?

A: A woman was baffled at her inability to find a favorite book in her home library. She finally realized her error. Weeks earlier she had removed the book's jacket, but her eyes were still seeking its color and design. The unjacketed book had been there all the time. In life, customary ideas prevent us from seeing the ever present truth.

708. Q: We spend our lives waiting for good

things to happen, which seldom do.

A: Something good is always happening within, which we miss without realizing what is missed. Take the opportunity to study the false cause of loneliness. Why not let an alert mind investigate? Would the end of loneliness be a good thing to happen?

709.   Q: I succeeded in an assignment you gave us last month. You said to observe the hostility of people toward rescuing facts.

A: A lost mind always tries to drag noble truth down to its own level, like a bat accusing an eagle of living in a dark cave.

710.   Q: Discuss the wrong and right way of seeing life.

A: You see yourself and life through your emotions, tastes, fears, ambitions, opinions and other distorting and limiting factors. You can also see the world with cosmic consciousness, which is above the self and which sees everything clearly, distorting nothing. An examination of the first way of seeing reveals the second way of seeing.

711.   Q: Help us to see something we need to see.

A: Those who work on themselves will eventually see the difference between the suppression of anxiety and the absence of anxiety, and with this insight they have no anxiety.

712.   Q: Tell us something we need to hear.

A: You cannot demand your own way and then demand that other people pay for the painful consequences of your way. The person who sets the cause into motion is the person who must pay for the effect. This is cosmic law.

713. Q: Please explain the law of cause and effect.

A: A teacher and his disciples were seated by the roadside when a troubled man who was known to the group walked by. A disciple asked the teacher, "Why does he experience so much misfortune?" Said the teacher, "It is very simple. His inner state is a disaster. He reproduces it outwardly wherever he goes."

714. Q: How can we avoid irresponsibility toward ourselves?

A: Observe the consequences.

715. Q: You mean consequences such as apprehension and feelings of doom?

A: There is no way to frighten an individual who has taken full responsibility for living his own life.

716. Q: The tyrant is my own unclear mind!

A: Thank heaven you see that at last. Now you can work intelligently to replace the tyrant with a cosmic king.

717. Q: Why do our activities produce so little of real value?

A: A visitor at a factory expressed awe at a huge machine that was noisily moving its wheels and arms. The foreman explained, "In spite of appearances it is doing nothing useful. It is a faulty machine we are trying to repair." What people call an active life is simply pointless agitation, a desperate attempt to prove themselves. But with spiritual repair, they can become productive.

718.　Q: Why do we stumble through life?

A: The answer is so simple you may miss it. We stumble only because we walk in darkness while insisting it is light.

719.　Q: Then our self-deception is also our punishment.

A: Anyone who chooses darkness over daylight must remember with whom he must live—with someone who has chosen darkness.

720.　Q: I see why the study of self-deception is essential.

A: Human beings are so self-deceived they actually believe that talking about virtue is the same as possessing it. Thieves find it easy to talk about honesty. Cruel minds chatter endlessly about love and kindness. Imagine a vagabond standing outside of a jewelry shop. He tells passers-by about his diamonds and emeralds and sapphires. That is humanity.

721.　Q: Does heaven really care for me?

A: It depends on who you are. Who are you?

722. Q: I don't know.
A: Find out. Discover at least a small part of you that represents heaven on earth. Then you will know whether or not heaven cares for you.

723. Q: How will I know?
A: When the bit of heaven in you calls out, Higher Heaven will answer.

724. Q: We need a better guide than our own opinions.
A: Do you know that honesty to oneself is a perfect guide? I will tell you a short story. There was once a man who finally arrived at the fountain of truth, and he started by knowing that he did not know.

725. Q: Please clarify the problem to us, so we might act intelligently toward it.
A: Man refuses to turn away from his fixation for fear there may be nothing other than his captivating trance. Imagine a small child fascinated by a colorful picture of a huge waterfall. You invite him to step outside to see the magnificent waterfall itself. But his attention is so fixed on the motionless picture he neither hears nor understands your invitation to view nature in action.

726. Q: Last week some of us fell into a discussion about normal and abnormal viewpoints. Please help us here.

A: The abnormal see everything from their own self-deceiving and self-flattering level, therefore the abnormal see the abnormal as normal and see the normal as abnormal. Only the normal can see the normal as normal and the abnormal as abnormal.

727. Q: We are grounded by our own artificiality?

A: Whoever lives from his real nature will soar. An orphaned eagle found himself flying with a flock of awkward geese. Believing himself to be a goose he tried to imitate the ways of the flock, but found it frustrating and impossible. One day he met another eagle who wisely told him about his actual nature. From that day on the eagle soared and lived like the eagle he was.

728. Q: It seems mysterious, but there must be an explanation of how right ideas appear to those who need them.

A: Real sincerity serves as a magnet to attract true teachings to the individual who sincerely wants them.

729. Q: Every day we are torn between various choices. How can we escape the tyrant of indecision?

A: Living in indecision means you are still living from the imaginary self. You strain to choose the most beneficial course but the next minute you are dismayed to find that the most beneficial course seems to be another direction. This leaves

you right back where you started, tired and per-
plexed.

730. Q: That describes it perfectly, but I still
don't understand.
    A: You are torn like this because the imagi-
nary self is always trying to promote and protect
itself, which is an impossible task. Can you protect
an imaginary home? No. A whole man is never
pained by indecision because he lives from his
cosmic nature which needs nothing outside of itself.

731. Q: What about those everyday decisions
which are necessary, as when shopping or doing
business?
    A: A free human being understands that
artificial man has created artificial social affairs
based on egotism and trickery. A free man makes
everyday choices based on this knowledge, which
makes him wise and efficient. He buys bread
because he needs bread, but never buys anything in
order to impress friends.

732. Q: How is rescuing Reality created?
    A: Our part is not to create Reality but to
reveal it by removing whatever blocks its view. It
is like tearing down an old building to gain the
permanent view of a colorful meadow.

733. Q: How are these cosmic secrets obtained?
    A: Diligent effort is necessary. There was
once a man who understood nature's secrets. He

was able to build a home in which sun and wind and rain were used to keep the home at a perfect temperature in all seasons. He was constantly visited by people who wished to learn his secrets, but they discovered that the master-builder spoke a different language. Therefore only those who made an effort to learn the language learned the secrets.

734.   Q: We need all the help we can find.

A: Just as a flower opens itself to sunshine, you receive more help the moment you increase your capacity to receive more help.

735.   Q: Can a right intention help here?

A: A good intention is a good start, but give it energy and direction by showing it cosmic facts.

736.   Q: For example?

A: Those who win cosmic self-success are those who do not mistake a new excitement or a new belief or a new environment for a new life.

737.   Q: What is the difference between suppressing a harmful thought and eliminating it?

A: A suppressed thought is unseen, unconscious, like a fox hiding in dark bushes. Elimination comes by seeing it clearly and without judgment, then dropping it deliberately. A suppressed thought will return, but a thought dropped consciously disappears from the mind.

738. Q: I have an intellectual grasp of these principles, but sense the need for something higher. What is this need?

A: Sooner or later you will *feel* the truth, like a shipwrecked swimmer who finally feels solid ground under his feet.

739. Q: I am wrongly involved with someone. What can be done?

A: Wrong involvement is caused by living from the false self. It always strays into wrong involvements and then wonders how to get out. Find your real self and wrong involvements cease. Also, your true nature knows the right way to handle your present wrong involvement.

740. Q: How can we break mechanical thinking?

A: Have you ever watched the face of someone lost in a daydream? He stares but at nothing. He does not know where he is. He will be a bit startled when spoken to. Try to catch yourself in this kind of mechanical thinking. Shake your head. Snap out of it. Deliberately awaken yourself.

741. Q: I used to think that almost everyone wanted to recover themselves, but no more. So is it possible to meet other people with cosmic aims?

A: Imagine yourself trying to find the right road leading to a magnificent castle. After many errors you finally set foot on it. It is certain that you will meet other people on the road, those who also sought and found it. You now have some real friends. You can help each other reach the castle.

742. Q: You are right in describing us as captives. I am often captured by distressing thoughts.

A: You can withdraw from distressing thoughts any time you wish. Just develop your cosmic talent for doing so. What greater talent could you want?

743. Q: Why do we live such artificial lives?

A: Because we live from artificial selves. But remember something. It is very difficult for anyone to see or accept the fact that he is living from an invented image of himself rather than from his real nature. This hardened image itself lets out the loudest scream of protest when a man wanders too close to this fact, for it does not want to lose its tyrannical hold on him. Only by taking his daily shocks rightly can a man begin to break up the tyranny of the artificial self.

744. Q: What is the right way to meet shocks?

A: Take every heartache or terror with a quiet wish to understand it thoroughly. This means we must abandon the false pleasure of resentment, self-pity, and must also drop the peculiar pleasure of fearing someone or something. In other words, make an effort to meet life consciously instead of with the usual mechanical reactions.

745. Q: How does this affect daily life?

A: You become like a wise boatman on the

river who knows how to avoid rocks because he once bumped and remembered.

746. Q: What is a wrong use of imagination?

A: There are multitudes of men and women who never venture up the path to the mountain peak because distorted imagination deludes them into thinking they are already up there.

747. Q: You mean they have only a surface religion?

A: Yes, an imaginary religion, and to prove it such people get angry and upset when told about it, though they may mask their nervousness behind a public show of politeness.

748. Q: Society's answers to human problems only make things worse. Why?

A: Simple and right answers are neither accepted nor understood by a society which lacks both simplicity and rightness. Suppose you ask, "What is the cause of war and crime?" The only right answer is, "The unconscious behavior of individuals who imagine they are conscious." But this is rejected because every man suspects that he himself is part of the madness but cannot admit it. So complicated and wrong answers are invented as evasions.

749. Q: So man cannot do anything for himself without first seeing what he is doing against himself?

A: A simple story illustrates the human plight. A man was sleeping at the cold and uncomfortable base of a mountain, while *dreaming he occupied the comfortable plateau.* Man dreams he is conscious, never permitting his pains to tell him otherwise. Man must awaken.

750. Q: Why do we handle everything so awkwardly?

A: Because past thought interferes with present awareness, ruining our competence at the present moment. Many automobile accidents happen because a strong idea overpowers the attention which should be on driving the car. It also happens any time you become upset because your plans did not succeed as desired. Live in the clearness of the present moment.

751. Q: How can we tell whether we really understand a situation involving other people?

A: You really understand when you are not negative toward it in any way, when not distressed, not resentful, not tense.

752. Q: I fail to understand why there are thousands of programs for social harmony but no harmony.

A: Imagine a mechanical robot which goes wild and wrecks the contents of a room. Now imagine its owner instructing it, "Repair the damage you have done." It would be foolish instruction, for a destructive machine cannot take

200

constructive action. Man is a psychic robot like this, which is why he cannot repair the wreck he has made of society. He can only rearrange the broken pieces, while calling it constructive action. Only a new nature can create a new room.

753. Q: What can I do about my own resistance to needed facts?

A: When resisting rescuing principles the wise course is to study your very resistance. Resistance is a false process which knowledge can expose.

754. Q: I feel unable to find the kingdom.

A: Refuse the feeling. Refuse it a thousand times. The fact is, we have temporarily misplaced the keys to the kingdom, but the kingdom itself is always there, awaiting our entrance.

755. Q: I will be returning soon to my home town where we have weekly classes in these principles. How can we uplift our meetings?

A: Sometime, instead of everyone asking many questions, discuss deeply the answer to a single question. Take the question, "How can we increase our loyalty to cosmic rightness?" See how much you can gain from this single question. I will give you a start. Loyalty is the sensing of being on the right road at last.

756. Q: Everything we do does nothing.

A: If we could just see the absurdity of what

we are trying to do! Using fallacy for getting through life instead of fact is like trying to find a substitute for air. Simply see the absurdity of trying to do the impossible. Then we can sensibly settle down to achieve the possible.

757.   Q: We seem to do everything but the necessary when it comes to self-rescue.

A: A man in internal warfare would give anything to get himself on his own side, but all he needs to give is a deep interest in cosmic principles.

758.   Q: In our heart of hearts we often feel that all is lost.

A: You believe that all is lost? That is a belief and nothing more. I don't accept that belief for you—not for one second. I will give you a fact for making that powerless belief fade like darkness before the sun. That fact is, all can be found, for you can be found. Never mind your belief; just take the available fact.

759.   Q: Others have succeeded, but can I?

A: The very same spiritual tools used by others to build their cosmic castles are also available to you. They include a yearning to know and a willingness to investigate.

760.   Q: It can be done?
A: It can be done.

TEN METHODS FOR DAILY VICTORY

a. Real inspiration comes by choosing the true.

b. Higher facts deliver authentic encouragement.

c. Cosmic insight enables you to see life rightly.

d. Sincerity is a magnet for attracting inner poise.

e. A whole mind is never pained by indecision.

f. Remove whatever blocks your view of the other world.

g. Wrong involvements fall away from an earnest seeker.

h. Break the tyranny of artificial personality.

i. See daily shocks as helpful lessons, not as enemies.

j. Be assured that you can reach the cosmic castle!

About
Vernon Howard

VERNON HOWARD is a unique teacher who has broken through to another world.   He sees through the illusion of suffering and fear and loneliness.

His books are widely used by doctors, psychologists, clergymen, educators, etc.   He shows you exactly how to end all problems.   Read his inspiring books and see for yourself!

VERNON HOWARD lives and teaches in Boulder City, Nevada.

Invitation

Please send us the names and addresses of friends who may be interested in these helpful teachings. We will send them our free literature.

Also, for your own information on books, tapes and classes write:

911 Bryant Place
Ojai, California 93023-3301
805-640-2777
Fax: 805-640-2772

Ojai, California 93024
(805) 933-1000

Discover the Wonderful World
of VERNON HOWARD

POWERFUL BOOKS
> Treasury of Positive Answers
> Psycho-Pictography
> The Power of Your Supermind
> The Mystic Masters Speak
> Inspire Yourself
> The Mystic Path to Cosmic Power
> There is a Way Out
> 1500 Ways to Escape the
>   Human Jungle
> Esoteric Mind Power

ENRICHING BOOKLETS
> 50 Ways to See Thru People
> Conquer Anxiety and Frustration
> Your Power to Say No
> Sex and Sweethearts
> 50 Ways to Get Help from God
> Women: 50 Ways to See Thru Men
> Be Safe in a Dangerous World
> Conquer Harmful Anger 100 Ways
> Live Above This Crazy World

NEW LIFE
PO Box 684
Boulder City, Nevada 89005

NEW LIFE
PO Box 2090
Ojai, California 93024